SPAIN

Recipes by **EMILY LYCOPOLUS**
Photos by **DL ACKEN**

SPAIN

RECIPES
FOR OLIVE OIL AND
VINEGAR LOVERS

TOUCHWOOD EDITIONS

CONTENTS

INTRODUCTION

The food of Spain is as varied, fascinating, and unique as the cultures that have influenced it over the centuries. You'll find some of the best seafood and land produce you could ever hope to taste, thanks to the country's amazingly diverse terrain and climate. But simplicity is also a major influence. The Spanish know that their local ingredients are so incredible that often they need to add only a light drizzle of olive oil, a touch of salt, or a few drops of vinegar to create a truly decadent dish.

The quality of the ingredients we can access in North America frequently doesn't compare to what is grown in the gardens and fields of Spain, and because of this, Spanish food is frequently overlooked on our continent. I know I'll never be able to fully re-create the first *pan con tomate* that Steve and I enjoyed in Girona on our first evening in Spain together, celebrating our first anniversary years ago, but in these pages, I've done my best to share recipes and a culture that I love dearly by using accessible ingredients while trying to preserve the traditional qualities. Buy the best-quality ingredients that you can. They'll give you the most delicious results.

You might know that Spain is a country that values eating together. The Spanish eat dinner later than anyone else in Europe (sometimes as late as midnight), and lunch, the largest meal of the day, is typically enjoyed in the early afternoon, with three or four courses usually eaten at home. Siesta, which may or may not include a nap, is still a real thing, and businesses typically shut down in the afternoon for several hours so that families can eat together at home. *Sobremesa* doesn't have a direct translation into English, which is significant. It literally means "over the table" (and also "tablecloth"!) and refers to the practice of staying at the table after all the tasty food has disappeared to sit and talk, keeping families and friends close and connected. If the conversation is good, a gin tonic or glass of sherry will appear. *Sobremesa* can last for hours. Many of us in North America, with our busy, stressful, technology dependent lives, could benefit from this.

For many North Americans, Spanish food means *tapas*. Because of the length of time between lunch and dinner, Spaniards often go bar-hopping after work and before dinner, enjoying a drink and a few tapas. One of the many stories about the origin of tapas is that they began as a way to occupy stagecoach drivers. Drivers would be served glasses of sherry, topped with a piece of *jamón* to prevent bugs from flying into the glass, and a wedge of cheese or bread while they waited for guests at a party. These small plates are known in the north of Spain as *pinchos* (*pintxos* in the Basque Region) and tapas in the south. Sometimes they're free, sometimes you have to pay for them; some are as simple as marinated olives or fried peppers and others are as complex as croquettes and braised meatballs. They're a very tasty part of Spanish cuisine and regional variations abound, but they offer only a very limited picture of the true cuisine of Spain. In these pages, you'll find not only some of my favorite tapas but also a variety of other Spanish-inspired main meals, side dishes, and cocktails.

Use the best ingredients you can, but remember the three key points for an authentic Spanish experience: simplicity, community, and conversation. Spain has perfected these, and they're most definitely evident in its cuisine.

EXTRA VIRGIN OLIVE OIL

By far the largest producer of olive oil globally, Spain truly is a titan in the olive oil world. Many of the varieties that we use today are Spanish in origin, including Picual, Arbequina, Hojiblanca, and Manzanillo. Each varietal is like a fine wine to be paired and enjoyed with specific dishes for specific occasions, and, of course, everyone has their own favorites. But whatever your favorite, a drizzle of fresh delicious olive oil on a piece of bread, tomato, or wedge of cheese indisputably changes the flavor in all the best ways. For each of the previous books in this series, I chose as key ingredients two infused olive oils that suit the country's cuisine best, but for *Spain*, one of the choices had to be the classic extra virgin olive oil (in a few different varietals), as it is so intertwined in the culture and cuisine and brings its own unique flavor to every dish.

Earthy and delicious, this infused olive oil is as bright as it is herbaceous and complements so many dishes from Spain. You'll find that you can fully incorporate it into a dish without overpowering the other ingredients. While it's certainly distinctive, it's also subtle, and it will soon become second nature to add a drop or two to perk up your recipes. A sprig of rosemary is traditionally added to many stocks and soups, chopped and incorporated into sauces, and used as a garnish, but the resulting flavor is often overpowering or uneven. The Rosemary infused olive oil tackles both those challenges and is now an essential ingredient in most Spanish-influenced recipes in my home.

ROSEMARY INFUSED OLIVE OIL

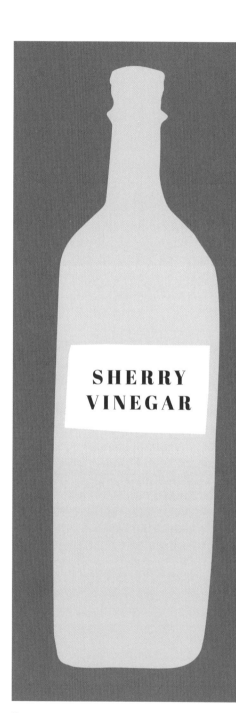

SHERRY VINEGAR

Sherry is a fascinating fortified wine. Like balsamic vinegar, it's aged via the solera method, where fresh wine is added to aging barrels, and flor, a layer of yeast spores, forms on top as the wine ages. The flor prevents oxygen coming into contact with the wine, and allows it to age in a biological or nonoxidative fashion. The sherry's dryness depends on how long the wine is left with the flor intact, although it's generally aged for a minimum of two years. Sherry vinegar is a traditional sherry that has undergone acidic fermentation and subsequently become a vinegar. The variation in Sherry vinegars is as broad as the variety of sherry available, so you might want to experiment with a few options. In this book, I've used a Pedro Ximénez, which is rich, sweet, and bright and adds so much flavor to the dishes I've included here for you to enjoy.

Citrus is in many ways as ubiquitous in Spain as olive oil, whether in the form of bright, juicy oranges, tasty, lip-puckering lemons, or whole grapefruits. Flavorful, zesty, and deliciously refreshing, a little goes a long way with this balsamic. It's perfect with fish, and it tempers the sweetness of honey in sauces and dressings. Try adding a splash of Grapefruit white balsamic vinegar to sparkling water for a refreshing drink on a hot day. Or bring some to a boil, toss in some shrimp or scallops, and watch it reduce and glaze them for a deliciously simple two-ingredient dish! Drizzle it over fruit or ice cream, whip it into yogurt to eat with granola, or add it to caramel sauce. I'd need an entire book just to discuss all the possible uses for this balsamic! Experiment and play with it, as it often finds its way into unexpectedly delicious places—and it's always enjoyed.

GRAPEFRUIT WHITE BALSAMIC VINEGAR

TAPAS

TOMATO BREAD
PAN CON TOMATE

The simplest of dishes somehow always ends up being the most delicious. It's generally believed that this Catalonian dish was originally created to liven up stale bread and use up extra-juicy tomatoes. A special bread called *pan de cristal* (literally, crystal bread), which has extra-airy pockets for more tomato-soaking-up potential, and tomatoes specifically grown for the express purpose of rubbing on freshly toasted bread are traditionally used for this in Catalonia, where it goes by the name *pa amb tomàquet*. The ingredient list is very small, so do use the best ingredients you can: homegrown or market-fresh tomatoes at the peak of ripeness, fresh bakery bread (I like a hearty sourdough for this), and the best extra virgin olive oil you can find (try Picual for a dish to remember!).

––––––––––––––––––

Preheat the broiler or grill.

Slice the bread or buns in half, toast well on each side, and drizzle each piece with ½ Tbsp of olive oil while they're hot. Rub a tomato half onto each piece, ensuring you get all the way to the edges, squishing as much flesh as you can into the toasted bread. Sprinkle with sea salt and enjoy immediately.

SERVES
FOUR
––––

4 large slices (each ¾–1 inch thick) bread, or square ciabatta buns

4 Tbsp robust extra virgin olive oil

4 fresh Roma tomatoes, halved

Sea salt

––––––––––

Keep the leftover tomato skins to add to vegetable stock for extra flavor and a touch of color.

There's much debate over whether the tomato should be cut in half and rubbed on the bread directly or grated, spooned onto the bread, and then rubbed in. To make everyone happy, I put a basket of freshly toasted bread, whole tomatoes, olive oil, sea salt, and a paring knife on the table so everyone can make their own. If I'm feeling adventurous, I'll add a bottle of Sherry vinegar and a few cloves of garlic to the table and let people play with different flavor combinations.

CROQUETTES

These tasty bar treats have so many variations and possibilities. The perfect combination of a crunchy, crispy, fried outside and creamy filling, they are rich and supremely delicious. They can be filled with salt cod, pork, chicken, spinach, potato, and even pine nuts, but the extra-thick, chilled béchamel sauce is nonnegotiable. The Rosemary infused olive oil adds a lovely herbaceous flavor to the béchamel sauce that infuses it completely without taking over, as a fresh herb might do.

———————

Line a plate with paper towel.

In a small frying pan, sauté the bacon ends without any oil until crisp and golden brown. Transfer them to the prepared plate to drain off the excess fat and set aside.

Warm the Rosemary infused olive oil in a heavy-bottomed saucepan over medium heat. Sauté the onions for 1–2 minutes, until softened. Sprinkle them with the salt and then continue to cook until the onions are translucent and just starting to turn golden. Turn down the heat to low and sprinkle the flour over the onions, stirring to combine and remove any lumps. Slowly pour in the milk, whisking constantly to keep it all smooth. Remove the pan from the heat and, using a wooden spoon, stir in the cheese until smooth and fully melted, and then stir in the bacon ends. Transfer this béchamel sauce to a shallow bowl and cover with plastic wrap, ensuring the plastic wrap is directly on the surface of the sauce, to prevent a skin from forming. Place in the fridge for 2 hours or up to overnight.

While the sauce is cooling, or when you are ready to serve, prepare a dredging station. In one shallow bowl, whisk the eggs; in a second shallow bowl, place the flour,

SERVES
SIX

Makes 20-24 croquettes

1 cup diced bacon ends

2 Tbsp Rosemary infused olive oil

¼ cup diced red onion

½ tsp sea salt

¼ cup all-purpose flour

1 cup whole (3.25%) milk

1 cup grated Manchego cheese, grated

2 eggs

1 cup all-purpose flour

1 tsp sea salt

¼ tsp smoked paprika

1½ cups Panko bread crumbs

Extra virgin olive oil for frying

salt, and paprika; and in a third shallow bowl, place the bread crumbs.

Line a cookie sheet with parchment paper. Line a wire rack with paper towel.

Scoop up 2 Tbsp of the chilled béchamel sauce and use your fingertips to form it into a ball. Roll the ball first in the flour mixture to evenly coat, then dip it in the egg, and, finally, roll it in the bread crumbs. Set on the prepared cookie sheet and repeat with the remaining sauce. Place in the fridge and chill, uncovered, for at least 1 hour, or up to overnight.

When ready to serve, preheat oven to 200°F. Heat 2 inches of olive oil in a heavy-bottomed saucepan over medium-high heat to 375°F. Fry the croquettes in batches of three or four, so you don't overcrowd the pan, until golden brown and crispy, about 2 minutes per side. Using a slotted spoon, remove from the oil and let sit on the prepared wire rack to drain any extra oil. Give the oil a minute or two to return to temperature between batches. Keep them warm in the oven while you cook each batch, and then serve immediately.

Serrano and Iberico ham are hard to find in North America and are very expensive. Thick-cut bacon or bacon ends are wonderful substitutes and more reasonably priced.

Croquettes can be made in advance and reheated in the oven, although they are best served straight from the hot oil. The béchamel can also be made in advance, formed into balls, and frozen before being breaded and fried. They will keep in the freezer like this for up to 2 months. Once cooked, they'll keep in an airtight container in the fridge for up to 3 days. If cooking the béchamel balls from frozen, ensure they are able to thaw fully before frying, although breading them while frozen is easiest.

To prevent your fingers from becoming too sticky while dredging or breading, keep one hand reserved for handling the dry ingredients and the other for the wet.

MEATBALLS in TOMATO SAUCE
ALBÓNDIGAS

Traditionally these meatballs call for half veal and half pork, which mixes an expensive meat with a cheaper one and allows the fat from the pork to permeate the very lean veal. You are more than welcome to use this mixture, but here I'm using beef and pork, which create a richer flavor to pair with the tomato sauce. This combination plus the milk-soaked bread crumbs ensures that the meatballs are supertender and soft. The Rosemary infused olive oil is the perfect complement to it all, rounding out the flavor and adding a soft herbed note to the dish.

———————————

Cover a wire rack with a couple of layers of paper towel.

In a mixing bowl, soak the bread crumbs in the milk while you cook the bacon.

In a large frying pan over medium-high heat, fry the two strips of bacon until very crispy, remove from the pan, and let cool completely, leaving any leftover bacon grease in the pan. Finely chop the bacon and set aside.

Pour the oil into the bowl with the bread crumbs and milk and fluff the now moist bread crumbs with a fork. Mix in the eggs, grated shallot, and minced garlic, and then mix in the beef and pork, and then finally the bacon bits. Mix well after each addition to ensure that the mixture is fully incorporated.

Form the meatball mixture into tablespoon-size balls. Do your best to make the balls seamless.

Place ½ inch of olive oil in the frying pan with the leftover bacon grease in it, place over medium-high heat, and fry the meatballs in batches of four or five, being careful not to overcrowd the pan so they brown evenly. Fry them, stirring occasionally to make sure they brown evenly, for 4–5 minutes. If they aren't fully cooked through, that's OK, as long as they're golden brown. Remove them

SERVES
FOUR
———

Meatballs
½ cup dried bread crumbs
2 Tbsp (1% or 2%) milk
2 strips of bacon
2 Tbsp Rosemary infused olive oil
2 eggs
1 small shallot, grated
2 cloves garlic, minced
¼ lb extra-lean ground beef
¼ lb ground pork
Extra virgin olive oil for frying

Tomato Sauce
1 small red onion
1 small red bell pepper
2 large Roma tomatoes
2 Tbsp Rosemary infused olive oil
½ cup chicken stock
4 saffron threads
½ tsp smoked paprika
1 sprig fresh thyme for garnish

from the pan and let sit on the prepared wire rack. Once all the meatballs are cooked, drain all but 2 Tbsp of the olive oil from the pan and then return all the meatballs to the pan.

To prepare the sauce, finely chop the onion, pepper, and tomatoes.

In a small saucepan over medium heat, warm the oil and then sauté the onion for 1–2 minutes, until just translucent. Add the peppers and tomatoes and sauté for an additional 3 minutes, until the vegetables are tender. Add the stock, saffron, and paprika, turn down the heat to low, and simmer, uncovered, for 5 minutes. Remove from the heat and allow to cool slightly. Place all the ingredients in a blender and blend to a smooth sauce.

Pour the tomato sauce over the meatballs and place the frying pan over medium heat. Cover and allow to simmer for 15 minutes, until hot and bubbling and the meatballs are fully cooked through.

Serve immediately with a garnish of fresh thyme.

You can store these in an airtight container in the fridge for up to 1 week, or freeze them for up to 3 months. The meatballs are best frozen separately from the sauce and assembled together once thawed.

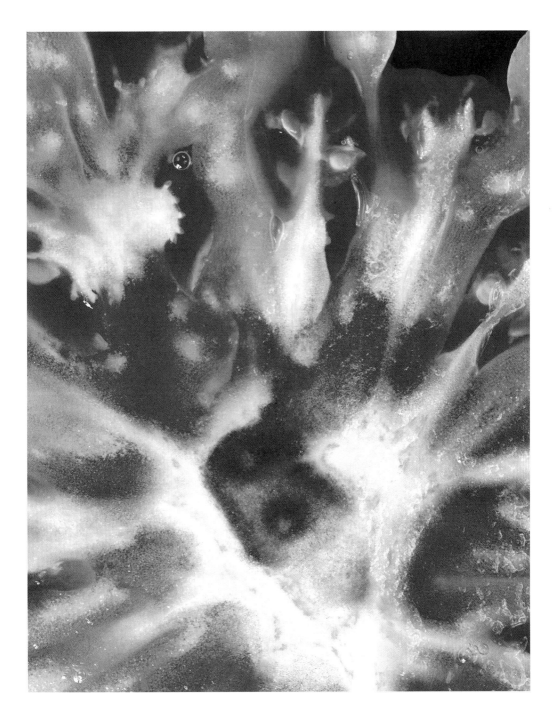

HOMEMADE CHORIZO COOKED
in CIDER *with* HONEY

Chorizo is the classic Iberian sausage. It comes in many forms—fresh, cured, semicured, spicy, and sweet—and is available for purchase in most butchers and grocery stores. However, just for fun, I've included a recipe here, so you can make it fresh at home, although you're more than welcome to substitute fresh chorizo from the store if making it from scratch is too time-consuming. The sausages here end up being more like little meatballs, since putting the sausage in casings is not necessary and home-curing sausage is not advised. The Rosemary infused olive oil makes for a lovely herbaceous flavor in among the spicy smokiness of the sausage and the sweetness of the honey and cider.

———————————

In a mixing bowl, mix together the pork, egg, bread crumbs, garlic, paprika, parsley, salt, vinegar, and the 1 Tbsp olive oil until fully combined. Form the mixture into 1-inch diameter disks, about ½ inch thick.

In a 10-inch frying pan, drizzle in more olive oil, 2–3 Tbsp depending on the size of the pan, and warm it over medium-high heat. Sear the small chorizo patties, in batches of three or four, for 2–3 minutes per side, until fully browned on both sides. There's no need to ensure that they're cooked through as they'll cook in the cider.

Add the cider to the pan and bring to a boil, then turn down the heat to medium-low and simmer, uncovered, for 15 minutes, turning the chorizo occasionally so they cook through evenly. The liquid will reduce as it cooks.

Place the chorizo in a shallow serving bowl, pour over any residue cider from the pan, and drizzle with honey. Garnish with fresh rosemary (if using).

You can store leftovers in an airtight container for up to 1 week in the fridge, or up to 3 months in the freezer.

SERVES
FOUR

1 lb ground pork

1 egg

½ cup dried bread crumbs

2 cloves garlic, minced

1 Tbsp smoked paprika

1 Tbsp chopped fresh curly parsley

1½ tsp sea salt

2 Tbsp Sherry vinegar

1 Tbsp Rosemary infused olive oil, plus extra for frying

2 cups apple cider

2 Tbsp honey

Chopped fresh rosemary for garnish (optional)

SPANISH TORTILLA
TORTILLA DE PATATAS

This classic dish is as simple as it is delicious. Serve with aioli, or chilled with a meat and cheese platter.

SERVES
SIX

Peel the potatoes and slice them thinly and evenly. (I use a mandoline set at ¹⁄₁₀ inch.) Slice the onion into rounds or half-moon shapes as thin as the potato slices. Preheat the oven to 350°F.

In a large ovenproof frying pan, heat the extra virgin olive oil over medium heat. Add the onions and then the potatoes. Sauté for 3–5 minutes, using tongs to flip the potatoes to ensure even cooking. When the onion is translucent but not brown and the potatoes are fork-tender, not falling apart, remove the frying pan from the heat and set aside. Allow the potatoes and onion to cool in the pan for 5–10 minutes while you prepare the eggs.

In a large bowl, whisk together the eggs, water, and Rosemary infused olive oil until light and frothy. Ease the potatoes and onions in the frying pan in a single layer. Pour the egg mixture over the top and sprinkle with salt and pepper to taste. Lift a few of the potatoes around the outside edges to ensure that the egg mixture has seeped underneath to coat the bottom of the pan.

Bake the egg mixture for 35–40 minutes, until the top is firm and a toothpick inserted in the center comes out dry with only a few potato crumbs on it. Remove the pan from the oven and run a knife or spatula around the outside of it to loosen the egg. Let rest for 10 minutes, then place a large serving platter or cutting board over the top of the frying pan; carefully (with oven mitts on!) flip the pan over to turn the tortilla onto the platter. Cut into wedges and serve warm.

This will keep in an airtight container in the fridge for up to 4 days. Reheat it in a 350°F oven for 10 minutes.

4 large potatoes (Yukon gold or russet are best for this)

1 white onion

½ cup extra virgin olive oil

8 eggs

1 Tbsp water

¼ cup Rosemary infused olive oil

Sea salt and cracked black pepper

Adding the water while whisking the eggs means they'll be light and fluffy after cooking. The steam creates air pockets, which in turn create an extra-fluffy texture. This is also a great way to scramble eggs.

FRIED PEPPERS
PIMIENTOS DE PADRÓN

These peppers are a tasty snack that I love to serve in the peak of summer, when peppers are at their best and the last thing I want to do is turn on the oven. These are incredible when made on the grill, although you won't be disappointed if you fry them on the stove. The key to success is finding the best peppers. Import stores are the best option, and, of course, farmers' markets in the summer. Look for the smallest sweet peppers you can find. And stems make great handles, so finding tiny peppers with long stems would be ideal. If not, long skinny sweet peppers, often called Italian peppers, are a good substitute. No matter the size, I still cook them whole. Larger peppers might need a little longer to cook (and a knife and fork to eat them!).

SERVES
FOUR

2 Tbsp extra virgin olive oil

2 Tbsp Rosemary infused olive oil

16 small sweet bell peppers, or 8 large ones

2 tsp coarse sea salt

In a frying pan over medium-high heat, warm both the olive oils. Add the peppers and then turn down the heat to medium, gently frying the peppers, turning them occasionally, for 7–10 minutes, until they are evenly crispy and brown on all sides and soft on the inside.

Place the peppers on a serving platter and sprinkle with sea salt.

These peppers don't reheat well, but if there are any leftovers, keep them in the fridge in an airtight container, then chop them to use in scrambled eggs, soup, or *sofrito*.

SHERRY-ROASTED WILD MUSHROOMS

Spain does love its mushrooms, and in the fall, there are plenty of fresh chanterelles, lobster, and oyster mushrooms to be found. Button mushrooms are just as rich and delicious, though, if wild ones are not to be found in your neighborhood. The Rosemary infused olive oil allows each mushroom to really show off it earthy qualities, while the Sherry vinegar adds a refreshing tartness. Slicing the garlic instead of mincing it means it caramelizes beautifully and gives you a garlic pop every few bites, without being overpowering, which keeps the dish exciting and flavorful.

2 cloves garlic

¼ cup Rosemary infused olive oil

1 lb wild or button mushrooms

3 Tbsp Sherry vinegar

1 tsp sea salt

1 tsp fresh lemon thyme leaves
for garnish

Preheat the oven to 350°F.

Slice the cloves of garlic as thinly as possible. A mandoline is ideal for keeping the slices even and extra-thin—just watch your fingers!

In a frying pan over medium heat, warm the olive oil and add the garlic in an even layer. Allow it to turn just slightly brown and soften. Remove from the pan with a slotted spoon and place in a deep-sided 7- × 11-inch roasting dish. Leave any residue oil in the pan.

If the mushrooms are large, slice them in half; if they're smaller, or if you're using button mushrooms, leave them whole. Working in batches so you don't overcrowd the pan, add the mushrooms to the pan, turn to coat well in the olive oil, and sear the outsides. Transfer the seared mushrooms to the roasting dish and repeat until all the mushrooms are browned. Pour the olive oil from the pan and the Sherry vinegar into the roasting dish, and sprinkle with the salt. Cover with a lid or aluminum foil, and bake for 20–25 minutes, until the mushrooms are tender.

Serve immediately with a garnish of fresh thyme leaves.

These keep in an airtight container in the fridge for 2–3 days, although they're best enjoyed immediately.

PATATAS BRAVAS

This dish actually has a patent, which is displayed in the restaurant Las Bravas in Madrid. Although the recipe is secret, variations are found all over Spain. Essentially, potatoes are the carrier for a delicious, spicy tomato sauce.

Preheat the oven to 375°F. Line a baking sheet with parchment paper. Bring a large pot of water to a boil.

Wash (but don't peel) the potatoes and chop them into 1-inch cubes. Place them in the boiling water and cook for 3–5 minutes, until just fork-tender. Drain and immediately rinse with cold water. Place the potatoes on the prepared baking sheet, and drizzle with ¼ cup of the olive oil, tossing gently to coat. Place in the oven and bake for 15 minutes, turning once to ensure the potatoes are evenly browning on all sides.

While the potatoes are cooking, crush the garlic clove and dice the shallot and chili pepper, removing the seeds. Place the remaining ¼ cup of olive oil in a frying pan over medium heat. Sauté the shallot for 1–2 minutes. Add the garlic and the chili, sauté for 1 minute longer, sprinkle with the salt to allow the mixture to sweat, and then continue to cook for another 2–3 minutes, until the mixture is tender and golden brown, but not burnt.

Add the Sherry vinegar, deglazing the pan and scraping any bits off the bottom. Sprinkle in the smoked paprika, then pour in the crushed tomatoes and Tabasco (if you're looking for even more spice). Stirring constantly, turn the heat down to low and allow the sauce to reduce until very thick and all the liquid has been absorbed, at least 10 minutes.

Place the roasted potatoes in the pan with the sauce and mix to evenly coat them. Serve immediately, with a dollop of mayonnaise or garlic aioli (page 115) if desired.

SERVES
FOUR

3 large baking potatoes
(russet or Yukon gold are best)

½ cup robust extra virgin
olive oil, divided

2 cloves garlic

1 shallot

1 chili pepper

1 tsp sea salt

2 Tbsp Sherry vinegar

1 tsp hot smoked paprika

¾ cup crushed tomatoes

½ tsp Tabasco/hot pepper sauce
(optional)

The cooked potatoes can be stored in an airtight container for up to 4 days in the fridge. Panfry them in a little olive oil over medium heat to warm them through. The sauce can be stored separately in an airtight container for up to 1 month in the fridge. You might need to add a drop of water when you're reheating it. Sometimes I'll make a big batch of the sauce and store it to add a bit of spice to other dishes or soups, a little like a spicy *sofrito*.

GRILLED GARLIC PRAWNS *with* CHILI
GAMBAS AL AJILLO

Simple and delicious, this dish is another perfect example of basic ingredients coming together in a perfect union in the pan. Feel free to adjust the amount of spice to taste: if you love spice, add a diced fresh chili pepper; for less spice, use just a pinch of dried chili as a garnish.

Crush and peel the cloves of garlic. Reserve four cloves, keeping them whole, and finely dice the remaining two.

In a large nonstick frying pan over medium heat, place the olive oil. Add the shrimp and the four whole cloves of garlic. Sprinkle with the paprika and chili flakes, and stir to combine.

Turn the shrimp over as soon as they turn pink, 20–30 seconds, and sear on the other side for 20–30 seconds.

Add the remaining garlic and sauté the shrimp until the garlic is just starting to turn golden brown. Add the Sherry vinegar and deglaze the pan, scraping any bits of garlic off the bottom. Continue to sauté for 10 more seconds, until the vinegar has reduced and glazed the garlic and shrimp.

Garnish with parsley (and more chili flakes, if desired) and serve immediately. These will keep in the fridge for up to 2 days in an airtight container. You can reheat them in a little oil to warm them through.

SERVES
FOUR

---

6 cloves garlic

¼ cup extra virgin olive oil

1 lb jumbo shrimp (tails still attached if possible)

1 tsp smoked or sweet paprika

1 tsp chili flakes, plus extra for garnish (optional)

2 Tbsp Sherry vinegar

Chopped fresh curly parsley for garnish

Using shrimp that still have the tails attached make this a lovely finger food–style tapa.

FRIED GOAT CHEESE *with*
GRAPEFRUIT HONEY REDUCTION

Honey grapefruit reduction is a lovely tart and sweet complement to earthy goat cheese. This simple tapa is a decadent Spanish version of the ever-popular mozzarella sticks served in pubs all over North America.

———————————

Slice the log of goat cheese into eight even-size pieces.

Prepare a dredging station. In one shallow bowl, whisk the egg; in a second shallow bowl, place the bread crumbs, flour, paprika, and salt. Dip each piece of cheese first in the bread-crumb mixture to lightly coat, then in the egg, and then in the bread-crumb mixture again to coat them evenly and completely.

Place on a cookie sheet and place in the freezer to chill for at least 1 hour.

Drizzle at least ¼ inch of olive oil into a frying pan and heat it to about 350°F over medium-high heat. Place the chilled goat cheese rounds in the pan, and fry until golden brown underneath, 2–3 minutes. Carefully turn the rounds and cook the other side until browned. You might need to do this in batches to avoid overcrowding the pan.

Place the cooked cheese on a serving plate.

In a small saucepan over medium heat, place the balsamic, honey, and salt. Bring to a boil and then immediately turn down the heat to low and simmer until the sauce has reduced and is slightly thickened and golden, 1–2 minutes. Immediately drizzle it over the cheese, sprinkle with paprika, and serve.

Once the fried cheese has been drizzled with the sauce it doesn't keep well, so it should be enjoyed immediately. However, you can make it ahead of time: either freeze the cheese rounds before frying, or fry and then freeze in an airtight container to be thawed and reheated later. The sauce can also be made ahead and reheated immediately before serving.

SERVES
FOUR

1 small log (4–6 oz) of
goat cheese, chilled

1 egg

1 cup Panko bread crumbs

½ cup flour

2 tsp smoked paprika

½ tsp sea salt

Extra virgin olive oil for frying

¼ cup Grapefruit white
balsamic vinegar

2 Tbsp honey

½ tsp sea salt

Paprika for garnish

GRILLED ONIONS with ROMESCO SAUCE

Romesco is such a versatile sauce—nutty and creamy, tangy and rich—and it adds a Spanish twist to anything it touches. I use it instead of cocktail sauce for shrimp cocktail, and instead of tartar sauce for fish and chips, roasted potatoes, or sweet potatoes. Feel free to substitute walnuts, pecans, hazelnuts, pine nuts, or a mixture, for the almonds. The Rosemary infused olive oil evens out the flavor and ensures that every bite is as good as the last!

Preheat the oven to 350°F.

Spread the almonds on a baking tray and roast for 10 minutes, until just turning golden.

In a blender or food processor, place the roasted almonds, the 2 Tbsp olive oil, vinegar, peppers, tomatoes, and garlic. Pulse a few times to combine, and then add the seasonings and blend until completely smooth. Scrape into a serving dish.

Heat a grill to high heat, or if using the oven, set out a roasting pan and preheat the oven to 375°F.

Slice the large onions into halves or quarters. Place the onions on the grill or in the roasting dish, brush with some olive oil, and drizzle a little into the slices to ensure the olive oil seeps in. Grill for 10–15 minutes, turning once, or bake for 25 minutes, covered with aluminum foil, until the onions are tender and the larger onions have started to fall open slightly.

If using the oven, turn on the broiler to high, remove the foil from the onions, and char the tops of the onions for 2–3 minutes, keeping a close eye on them so they don't burn.

Serve immediately with the Romesco sauce on the side for dipping.

The Romesco sauce can be stored in an airtight container in the fridge for up to 1 week, but the onions should be enjoyed the day they are made.

SERVES
FOUR

½ cup whole blanched almonds

2 Tbsp Rosemary infused olive oil, plus extra for drizzling

2 Tbsp Sherry vinegar

4 roasted red bell peppers

2 Roma tomatoes, roughly chopped

2 cloves garlic, crushed

½ tsp smoked paprika

Pinch ground cumin

Chili flakes, sea salt, and cracked black pepper to taste

4-6 onions (a variety of red, white, and green/spring, and cipollini if you can find them)

MARINATED OLIVES

In many ways, olives are the foundation of Spanish cuisine. Whether as whole olives or, more often, in their juice form, brined olives appear on every table. In North America, it is challenging to find freshly picked, unbrined olives even in olive-growing regions, so this recipe calls for prepared olives. However, if you can find fresh ones, feel free to try brining them yourself at home. They will be crunchy and delicious, although they usually take between 12 and 18 months to cure, so there's a bit of a time commitment if you choose that option!

Makes 4 cups

2 cups brined whole olives

1 red bell pepper

6-8 caper berries (optional)

8 cloves garlic

½ fresh lemon

1 Tbsp sea salt

1 cup Sherry vinegar

Wash and rinse the olives, place them in a mixing bowl.

Seed and roughly chop the pepper, and add it to the mixing bowl with the caper berries.

Crush the cloves of garlic with the back of a knife, remove the skin, and place the squished whole cloves in the bowl. Slice the lemon in half lengthwise, then cut each half into half-moons, removing any seeds, and add to the bowl. Sprinkle with salt, and toss well to evenly coat.

Place the olive mixture in a 1-quart mason jar, ensuring that all the ingredients are evenly dispersed. Top the jar with the Sherry vinegar. Let sit in the fridge for at least 12 hours or overnight.

Serve as a tapa with fresh bread, pan con tomate (page 13), cheese, and cured meats. It can be kept in an airtight container in the fridge for up to 3 months.

A mix of olives is lovely. Try mixing and matching Cerignola, Manzanilla, Hojiblanca, Castelvetrano, and Arbequina.

ROASTED ALMONDS

The perfect pre- or post-dinner snack, these roasted almonds can be made ahead and stored in an airtight container for weeks, although they are incredible served warm. These are typically served as a complimentary bar snack or tapa to encourage patrons to eat more, although they are also served at home. Tapas as we know them today were typically not served at home; instead, appetizers served at home were traditionally simple snack foods that don't require cooking. At home these almonds would be served alongside serrano ham, cured chorizo, and an assortment of cheeses and maybe some quince jelly and marinated olives (page 39).

SERVES
FOUR

1 cup blanched whole almonds

¼ cup Rosemary infused olive oil

2 tsp sea salt

1 tsp smoked paprika

Freshly chopped rosemary
for garnish (optional)

Preheat the oven to 325°F. Line a baking sheet with parchment paper.

In a mixing bowl, toss the blanched almonds with the olive oil until evenly coated. Add the salt and paprika and mix until the spices evenly coat the almonds.

Pour the almonds onto the prepared baking sheet in an even layer. Drizzle any residue olive oil and spices from the bowl over the top.

Roast the almonds for 15 minutes, until golden. Shake the pan, turn the almonds so they can roast evenly on both sides, and then cook for an additional 10 minutes, until they're evenly roasted and sizzling. Remove from the oven and allow to cool slightly before serving. Garnish with rosemary (if using).

These will keep in an airtight container for up to 2 months.

SOUPS

&

SALADS

GAZPACHO

This classic Spanish cold tomato soup really is the ultimate refreshing summer dish. Depending on how hot it is outside, and when I'm going to serve it, I'll add some ice cubes to the blender, creating a savory slushy for lack of a better description. The colder this soup and the hotter the weather the better it is.

———————————

Roughly chop the tomatoes, seed and chop the pepper, peel and chop the cucumber, peel and roughly chop the onion, and crush the garlic cloves.

Place the vegetables, vinegar, and parsley in the blender with 2 Tbsp of the olive oil, and blend until extremely smooth. If needed or desired, add 4–5 ice cubes to the blender and blend again to crush the ice.

Divide among four soup bowls, drizzle the remaining olive oil as a garnish, and serve immediately.

This will keep in an airtight container for up to 1 week, or in the freezer for up to 3 months.

SERVES
FOUR
———

4 large tomatoes

1 red bell pepper

1 English cucumber

1 small red onion

2 cloves garlic

2 Tbsp Sherry vinegar

1 Tbsp chopped fresh curly or flat-leaf parsley

¼ cup extra virgin olive oil, divided

TOMATO and BREAD SOUP
SALMOREJO

This Córdoba-style gazpacho is similar to traditional gazpacho, but includes bread to make the soup even thicker and richer than the traditional version, and it's topped with chopped bacon and hard-boiled eggs. Some recipes use as much bread as they do tomatoes to make it a thick sauce, others use only one or two slices to keep it more soup-like, and others top the soup with tuna rather than ham. The variations are many, but the final result is a thick, refreshing, and hearty soup, an odd combination that makes it so delicious and unique.

Roughly tear the bread and chop the tomatoes, garlic, and onion. Place them in a blender, add the remaining soup ingredients, and blend until very smooth.

Place the blender jug in the fridge for at least 3 hours before serving.

When you're ready to serve, prepare the garnish. Fry the bacon, let cool slightly, and crumble each piece and slice the eggs into rounds.

Pour the soup into bowls and top with crumbled bacon, slices of egg, and a drizzle of olive oil.

This will keep in an airtight container for up to 1 week in the fridge or in the freezer for up to 3 months.

SERVES
FOUR

Soup

4 slices (each ½–¾-inch thick) day-old white bread, crusts removed

4 large tomatoes (beefsteak are perfect)

2 cloves garlic

1 small red onion

⅓ cup Sherry vinegar

¼ cup extra virgin olive oil

2 Tbsp Rosemary infused olive oil

1 tsp granulated sugar

6 ice cubes

Sea salt and cracked black pepper

Garnish

4 slices of bacon

2 hard-boiled eggs

Rosemary infused olive oil

1 sprig fresh parsley or rosemary, chopped

BASQUE-STYLE TUNA SOUP with SOFRITO
MARMITAKO

Mixing spices and vegetables and then cooking them down to almost a paste in olive oil creates a lovely mellow rich base for soups and sauces. This base is called *sofrito*, and it's perfect in this simple fish soup. Traditionally made with the catch of the day—often cod or tuna—it was made on board fishing vessels. Those from the Basque Region know how to eat well, even on the high seas. Using the Rosemary infused olive oil in the *sofrito* imparts a delicious richness to the soup, and drizzling some extra virgin olive oil over the top creates the perfect finish.

―――――――――――

To prepare the *sofrito*, peel, smash, and finely chop the garlic. Peel and mince the onion, seed and chop the bell peppers, and seed and chop two of the tomatoes.

In a large heavy-bottomed soup pot over medium heat (I love to use a Dutch oven for this), sauté the garlic and onion in the olive oil for 2–3 minutes, until just translucent. Add the bell peppers and sauté for an additional 2 minutes. Add the chopped tomatoes, salt, parsley, and paprika, mixing well to coat the vegetables with the paprika. Turn down the heat to low and allow the vegetables to cook, covered, for 30 minutes to soften them completely.

While the *sofrito* is cooking, peel the potatoes and chop them into 1-inch cubes, seed and finely chop the remaining tomatoes, peel the carrot (leaving it whole), and wash and trim the leek (leaving it whole as well).

Uncover the pot, increase the heat to medium-high, stir in the Sherry vinegar, and boil off any extra liquid that might have formed in the pot, so the vegetables are almost paste-like in the pot. Add the potatoes, searing them gently for about 2 minutes, and add then add the remaining tomatoes. Cook for 2–3 more minutes, then

SERVES
FOUR
―――

4 cloves garlic

1 large red onion

3 red bell peppers

2 green bell peppers

6 Roma tomatoes

¼ cup Rosemary infused olive oil

½ tsp sea salt

1 Tbsp chopped fresh
flat-leaf parsley

1 Tbsp sweet paprika

4 large red potatoes

1 large carrot

1 leek

2 Tbsp Sherry vinegar

8 cups fish or vegetable stock

1 chili pepper

10 black peppercorns

1 lb tuna steak

Fresh crusty bread for serving

Sea salt and ground black pepper

add the stock to the pot and stir to combine. Add the carrot, leek, whole chili, and peppercorns to the broth. Turn down the heat to low and cook, covered, for 15 minutes, until the potatoes are just fork-tender.

Cut the tuna steak into bite-size pieces. Add it to the pot as soon as the potatoes are just tender and remove the carrot, leek, chili, and peppercorns. Simmer, uncovered, for an additional 5 minutes, and then serve with freshly toasted bread, salt and pepper to taste, and a drizzle of olive oil for garnish.

Sofrito can be made in advance and stored in the fridge for up to 1 month. Try adding a spoonful to soups and sauces as you would a homemade vegetable bouillon cube for a lovely special something on weeknights.

SPANISH STEW
COCIDO

Cocido literally means "cooked" but it also means "stew," and it's often translated as "meal in a pot." (Think of it as a Spanish cassoulet.) Almost every region in Spain has its own version of this traditionally chickpea-based comfort food, which was brought to Spain by the Moors. It's now made with meat and vegetables, and is considered by some to be a national dish. Traditionally, even though everything is cooked in the same pot, the stew is served in different courses: first the broth on its own, then the chickpeas and vegetables, and then the meat to finish. Serve this with fresh crusty bread on the side to sop up the leftover juices.

———

In a large saucepan over medium heat, place the onion and olive oil. Sauté for 2–3 minutes, until translucent, then add the pork belly, searing it for 1–2 minutes per side. Add the chicken legs, searing for 3–4 minutes per side, then add the chuck roast. Brown the beef, add the Sherry vinegar, scraping any bits off the bottom of the pot, and then add the chicken stock and chorizo. Bring to a simmer, then cover, turn down the heat to low, and simmer for 1 hour, until the meat is cooked through.

Add the chickpeas. Peel the carrots and chop them into 1-inch lengths. Scrub the potatoes and cut them into about 1-inch cubes. Add the carrots and potatoes to the pot along with the cabbage. Simmer, still on low heat, for an additional 45 minutes, until the vegetables are fork-tender and cooked through.

Remove the pot from the heat and prepare serving platters. Remove all the meats first, and place them on the first platter, cutting the beef into slices and the sausages into halves or thirds. Place the carrots, potatoes, and cabbage on the next platter, garnishing with about 1 Tbsp of olive oil, a drizzle of broth from the pot, and some

SERVES
FOUR

as a three-course meal

1 red onion, diced

¼ cup Rosemary infused olive oil, plus extra for garnish

4 slices of pork belly

4 chicken legs

½ lb whole beef chuck roast

2 Tbsp Sherry vinegar

8 cups chicken stock

2 large fresh chorizo sausages

2 (19 oz) cans of chickpeas, drained and rinsed

2 large carrots

2 potatoes (russet or Yukon gold are best)

2 cups roughly chopped green cabbage leaves

Fresh curly parsley for garnish

parsley. Drain the chickpeas from the broth, place them on the last serving platter with a little bit of broth to keep them warm, and garnish with some parsley. Pour the broth into a large soup bowl. Serve!

You can store each component in separate airtight containers in the fridge for up to 1 week. Freeze the cooked stock in an airtight container for up to 3 months.

Sometimes fine angel-hair pasta is added to the broth before serving. If you want to try this, after the broth has been drained, bring to a boil and add the pasta, cooking until just tender, then remove from the heat and serve.

BEAN and PORK SOUP
FABADA

Home-cooked comfort food at its finest, this Asturian stew is popular all over Spain. Normally I use canned beans in recipes, but here dried beans are a must for their nutty smoky flavor. The stew is ideal for a slow cooker, and you can leave it to cook overnight to ensure that the beans are cooked through and tender. Use the freshest dried beans possible—Great Northern, lima, and white kidney beans work well—to minimize the risk of splitting.

———————

Rinse the beans, place them in a large bowl of cold water, and soak for at least 3 hours.

Place the olive oil in a frying pan over medium heat. Add the onions and sauté for 2–3 minutes, until translucent. Sprinkle with sea salt to allow them to sweat. Cook, stirring, for 1 more minute and then transfer them to the bowl of a slow cooker. Add the cloves of crushed garlic. Drain the beans and add to the slow cooker.

In the frying pan, sear the sausages on medium-high heat to brown on all sides, then place on a cutting board to cool slightly while you sear the slab bacon. Place any drippings in the slow cooker. Chop the sausage into 1–2-inch pieces and the slab bacon into 1–2-inch chunks and place in them in the slow cooker. Add the ham hock, then add water to fill the slow cooker pot to within 1 inch of the top. Add the herbs and seasonings, then turn the slow cooker to low and cook for 8–10 hours, or until the beans are tender and the meat is cooked through.

When ready to serve, remove the sprigs of rosemary and thyme and the bay leaf. Spoon the stew into serving bowls and garnish with a drizzle of olive oil and extra paprika if desired.

This will keep in an airtight container for up to 1 week in the fridge. You can also freeze the broth and beans together (without the meat) for up to 3 months.

SERVES
FOUR
———

1 lb white beans

2 Tbsp extra virgin olive oil, plus extra for garnish

1 small white onion, diced

1 tsp sea salt

4 cloves garlic, crushed but whole

4 links chorizo sausage

½-lb slab bacon or pork belly

1 lb ham hock

2 sprigs fresh thyme

1 sprig fresh rosemary

1 bay leaf

½ tsp smoked paprika, plus extra for garnish

Pinch saffron threads

BEAN and POTATO SOUP
CALDO

Typically, the key to this dish the smoked salt pork, which adds a wonderful complexity. Traditional recipes for this specific dish don't tend to vary greatly, although one ingredient that is a source of contention is the chorizo. I've used it here, as finding smoked salt pork that's been cured beside a fireplace isn't easy in North America—and the soup just isn't the same without it. A splash of Rosemary infused olive oil adds an earthy rich quality to the soup and the Sherry vinegar keeps it tart and fresh. Traditionally, turnip greens were used in this, but cabbage, spinach, Swiss chard, and collard greens are all delicious, too.

SERVES
FOUR

2 cloves garlic

1 leek

6-8 stems of greens

2 Tbsp Rosemary infused olive oil

6 cups chicken stock

¼ lb pork belly

4 links chorizo sausage

2 large potatoes (Yukon gold or red work well)

1 (19 oz) can navy beans

Crush and mince the garlic, then wash and trim the leek and slice it into ¼-inch-thick rounds. Remove the large stems from the greens and roughly chop them, setting the greens tops aside.

In a large heavy-bottomed pot over medium heat, sauté the garlic, leek, and greens tops in the olive oil for about 5 minutes, until translucent but not brown.

Add the chicken stock and bring to a simmer. Pierce the pork belly and sausages a few times and then place them, whole, in the pot. Bring just to a boil and then turn down the heat, cover, and simmer for 1 hour.

While the soup is cooking, peel the potatoes and cut them into 1-inch pieces. Roughly chop the greens stems and rinse the beans.

Uncover the pot and remove the pork belly and the sausages. Cool slightly, then slice into bite-size pieces. Return the meat to the pot along with the potatoes, greens, and beans. Bring just to a boil over medium heat, then turn down the heat to medium-low, and simmer gently for 20–30 minutes, until the potatoes are just fork-tender.

Serve immediately, with about 1 Tbsp olive oil for garnish.

SPANISH-STYLE CHOPPED SALAD
VINAGRETA

The dressing on this salad is quite different from the very vinegar- and mustard-heavy French-style vinaigrette you might be more familiar with. Typically, this dish includes diced ingredients, from tomatoes, garlic, and cucumber to boiled egg. It's often served over blanched vegetables, grilled fish, or even cold roasted potatoes, but I love it served on a wedge of iceberg (yes, iceberg!) lettuce, allowing the little bits to essentially become the salad topping and to seep into the folds of the lettuce as well. This makes a refreshing lunch on a hot summer day, served with a chilled bowl of gazpacho (page 45) and fresh crusty bread.

———————————

Dice the tomatoes, onion, and egg very finely. Place them in a small mixing bowl and add the cucumber. Destem the thyme and rosemary, lightly chop them, and add them to the diced vegetables along with the parsley. Pour in the olive oil, vinegar, and honey and mix until fully combined. Add salt and pepper to taste.

Slice a head of iceberg lettuce into quarters and lay each quarter on its side on a serving plate. Pour one-quarter of the dressing over each slice, ensuring that lots of the diced veggies and egg land on top of the wedge and the dressing runs between the layers.

Serve immediately. The salad itself doesn't keep well, although the dressing can be kept in an airtight container for up to 3 days in the fridge.

SERVES
FOUR
———

2 small tomatoes on the vine

1 red onion

1 hard-boiled egg

½ cup diced English cucumber, skin on

2 sprigs fresh thyme

1 sprig fresh rosemary

2 Tbsp chopped fresh curly parsley

¼ cup extra virgin olive oil

¼ cup Sherry vinegar

1 Tbsp honey

Sea salt and cracked black pepper

1 head of iceberg lettuce

RUSSIAN POTATO and TUNA SALAD
ᴇNSALADA RUSA

There are many stories explaining how Russian salad landed in Spain and became a favorite salad served all over the country. It's especially popular in Galicia, where tuna is ever plentiful. The tangy mayo-laden dressing isn't only tasty, it also keeps the tuna preserved so it will keep in the fridge for a few days—and honestly, this is at its best the day after it's made, once the flavors have had time to meld and develop. Using the Rosemary infused olive oil and Sherry vinegar combines flavors beautifully and saves you from having to add fresh herbs.

––––––––––––––––

Slice the potatoes in half and peel and chop the carrots into coins.

Bring a pot of water to a boil over high heat, add the carrots and potatoes and boil, uncovered, for 10 minutes, until the vegetables are fork-tender and cooked through. Drain and run under cold water to stop them from cooking further and set aside to cool completely.

In a large mixing bowl, whisk together the mayo, olive oil, vinegar, mustard, salt, and pepper to fully combine.

Drain the tuna and flake it into the dressing along with the cooled potatoes, carrots, and peas.

Chop the pepper and add it to the bowl, mixing again to combine. Finally, add the olives. Let sit, covered, in the fridge for 1–2 hours to allow the flavors to develop. When you're ready to serve, transfer the salad to a serving bowl and garnish with sliced hard-boiled egg and green onions.

This will keep in an airtight container in the fridge for 2–3 days.

SERVES
FOUR
––––––

1 lb baby potatoes

2 medium carrots

½ cup full-fat mayonnaise

¼ cup Rosemary infused olive oil

¼ cup Sherry vinegar

2 tsp Dijon mustard

1 tsp sea salt

½ tsp cracked black pepper

1 (5½ oz) can tuna packed
in water

½ cup peas, fresh or frozen
and thawed

1 red bell pepper

¼ cup sliced pitted green olives

1 hard-boiled egg for garnish

2 Tbsp chopped green onions
for garnish

ROASTED TOMATO SALAD

This salad is unique and very distinctive thanks to the combination of the cumin seeds (a Moorish influence) and smoked paprika (a Spanish touch). This is often served with fresh tomatoes, but I love the added sweetness that roasting the tomatoes gives. The Rosemary infused olive oil lends a lovely earthy quality to the salad and really sets it apart.

————————————

Preheat the oven to 375°F. Line a rimmed baking tray with parchment paper.

Slice the tomatoes in half and place them cut side up on the prepared baking tray.

Drizzle the tomatoes with the olive oil and vinegar. Gently grind the cumin seeds in a mortar and pestle, then sprinkle them over the tomatoes, along with the paprika and salt.

Roast for 25–30 minutes, until the tomatoes are tender and blistering. Remove tomatoes from the oven and allow to cool completely.

Transfer the tomatoes to a serving platter, garnish with black olives and capers, drizzle with any leftover juices from the baking tray, and serve.

These will keep in an airtight container in the fridge for 2–3 days. Leftovers are lovely added to scrambled eggs for breakfast or whisked into a tomato sauce for pasta.

SERVES
FOUR
————

8 Roma tomatoes
¼ cup Rosemary infused olive oil
2 Tbsp Sherry vinegar
1 tsp toasted cumin seeds
½ tsp smoked paprika
½ tsp sea salt
½ cup pitted black olives
1 Tbsp capers

ENDIVE and CITRUS TWO-BITE SALAD CUPS

Another refreshing favorite, this not-quite-salad is the perfect summer barbecue finger food. It does take a bit of time to segment all the citrus, but it's so worth it. For an extra-special salad, use blood oranges if they're in season. The vinegar and leftover juices from the citrus create a simple tart dressing that complements the bitterness of the endive perfectly, and the sweetness from the honey rounds out the flavor, creating the most refreshing two-bite salad cups ever.

———————————

To segment the citrus fruit, slice the top and bottom of the fruit so a little flesh is exposed and set the cut side down on a cutting board. With a sharp paring knife, cut the peel off the orange, working from top to bottom, to expose the fruit inside. Turning the fruit so the segments are parallel to the cutting board, gently slice in between the membrane and the fruit on both sides of the membrane for each segment. Once cut, the segment should slide easily away from the membrane. Slice each segment into small wedges—I usually quarter them—with smaller pieces for the lime and larger pieces for the grapefruit and orange.

Slice the bottom off the endive and gently separate the leaves, laying them out on a serving platter so they look like little cups.

Evenly distribute the citrus fruit between the cups, top with thyme, then drizzle with vinegar, olive oil, and honey. Sprinkle with salt to taste and serve immediately.

These don't keep, unfortunately, and need to be enjoyed as soon as they are made.

SERVES
FOUR
———

1 orange

1 lime

1 ruby grapefruit

2 whole endive heads

2 sprigs fresh thyme

2 Tbsp Sherry vinegar

2 Tbsp olive oil

1 Tbsp honey

Sea salt

MAINS
&
SIDES

BAKED RICE and BEANS
ARROZ AL HORNO CON PASAS Y FRIJOLES

Rice and beans, possibly the simplest of dishes, is consumed in our house at least once a week. The combination of soft flavorful beans and moist grains of rice is just comfort in a bowl. This Spanish take is so easy, as it is cooked and baked in the oven in a shallow casserole dish called a *cazuela*, similar to a Dutch oven. Most Spanish rice dishes, including this one, originate from Valencia. This traditionally uses the broth leftovers from Cocido (page 54), although here chicken broth is used for simplicity. That said, if you happen to make Cocido, do save the broth as it takes any rice dish to another level of deliciousness. The citrus elements in my version of this dish make it a lovely combination of sweet and savory.

———

Place the currants and raisins in a small bowl. In a small saucepan, gently heat the orange juice over medium heat until it is almost boiling—moving gently in the pot, but not actually bubbling. Pour it over the currants and raisins and allow them to soak for at least 1 hour, or up to overnight.

Place the chicken stock and saffron in a large stockpot and bring to a simmer over medium heat to just warm the stock.

Preheat the oven to 400°F.

Finely chop the onion and two garlic cloves.

Warm the olive oil in a large ovenproof frying pan or Dutch oven over medium-high heat. Add the onions and garlic and sauté for 2–3 minutes, until translucent. Sprinkle the salt over the top to allow the onions to start sweating, then sprinkle in the paprika, stir to ensure that the onions are fully coated in the spice, and then add the balsamic to deglaze the pan. Scrape any bits of onion or garlic off the bottom. Gently crush the tomatoes with your hands as you add them to the pan, stirring well. Bring them to a simmer,

SERVES
EIGHT

½ cup currants

½ cup golden raisins

1 cup orange juice

4 cups chicken stock

3-4 strands of saffron

1 sweet onion

2 cloves garlic, plus 1 head

2 Tbsp extra virgin olive oil

1 tsp sea salt

1½ tsp sweet paprika

2 Tbsp Grapefruit white balsamic vinegar

1 (19 oz) can plum tomatoes, with juice

1 (19 oz) can black beans, drained and rinsed

1 (19 oz) can chickpeas, drained and rinsed

2 cups short-grain rice

uncovered, and let cook for 5 minutes to allow some of the juice to evaporate.

Drain the currants and raisins and add half of them to the sauce along with the beans and chickpeas. Stir to fully incorporate and allow to simmer for another 5 minutes to form a thick sauce. Add the rice and stir to combine. Pour in the warm stock, and then sprinkle the remaining currants and raisins over the top of everything. Finally, peel some of the outer skin off the head of garlic but not enough to fully expose any of the cloves. Place the whole head of garlic in the center of the pan. Carefully place it in the oven and bake for 30–35 minutes, uncovered, until the rice is tender and the liquid has completely evaporated. Remove from the oven and let sit for 5 minutes before serving.

To serve, break apart the head of garlic for each person to squeeze a clove onto their rice and beans.

Any leftovers will keep in an airtight container in the fridge for up to 1 week.

This dish makes a lot, so it's perfect for a winter dinner party, or a hearty meal with leftovers for the week. It doesn't divide or half well, but it does store well in the fridge.

If you don't have a pan that can both cook on a stovetop and then bake in the oven, cook the dish to the point of adding the rice, then transfer the contents of the pan to a 9- × 13-inch baking dish, add the stock, and bake, uncovered, as directed.

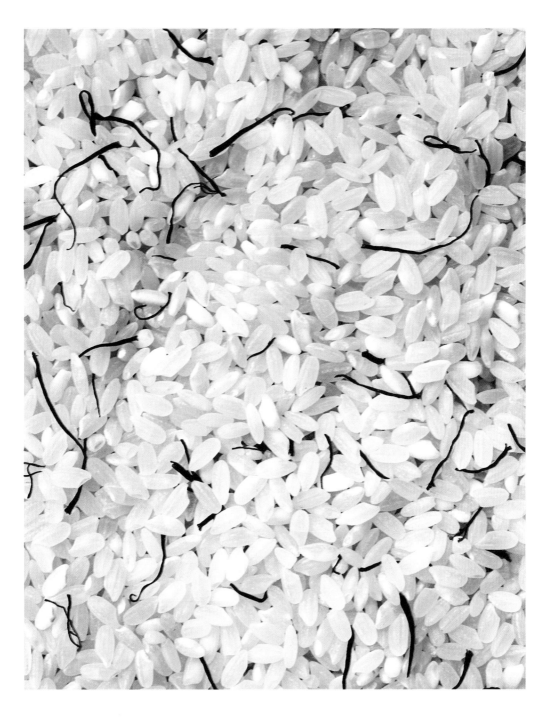

ROASTED EGGPLANT with CHEESE
BERENJENA CON QUESO

Eggplants and cheese is a traditional dish for the Jewish community in Catalonia. According to the archives, during the Inquisition, the inquisitors would look carefully at how people were cooking their food to see if they were continuing to secretly practice Judaism while claiming to have converted to Catholicism. This was a dark period in Spanish history, but some beautiful recipes evolved during this time and, because of meticulous record keeping, there is an amazing repository of food and recipe information from the era.

Slice the eggplant into 1–1½-inch-thick rounds. Place two or three sheets of paper towel on a cutting board or baking sheet and sprinkle with a little of the salt. Place the eggplant rounds on the paper towel, sprinkle with the remaining sea salt, and then cover with more paper towel. Let stand for 20–30 minutes to allow the water to drain from the eggplant.

Preheat the oven to 375°F. Bring a large saucepan of water to a boil.

Set the eggplant slices on a splash guard or in a flat-bottomed strainer. Steam them for 3–4 minutes, until just soft and tender. Ensure that the eggplant doesn't touch the water. Carefully place the eggplant in a single layer in the bottom of a baking dish or roasting pan.

While the eggplant is resting, bring the milk and cream to a simmer in a small saucepan over medium heat.

In a frying pan or heavy-bottomed saucepan over medium heat, warm the ¼ cup of olive oil and then add the onion. Sauté for 2 minutes, until the onion is just translucent but not brown. Add the flour and stir to get rid of any lumps and form a loose paste. It will bubble up a little—that's OK. Gently pour the warmed milk mixture into

SERVES
FOUR

1 large eggplant

2 Tbsp sea salt

¾ cup 2% milk

½ cup whipping (35%) cream

¼ cup + 2 Tbsp Rosemary infused olive oil, divided

1 small white onion, finely chopped

2 Tbsp all-purpose flour

1 cup grated mozzarella cheese

½ cup Panko bread crumbs

2 cloves garlic, crushed

¼ cup chopped fresh curly parsley

2 tsp fresh thyme leaves

Sea salt and cracked black pepper

½ cup grated Manchego cheese

the paste a little at a time, stirring constantly to prevent any lumps from forming and allowing the sauce to begin to thicken. Turn down the heat to low, and continue to stir for 2–3 minutes, until the sauce is fully combined. Add the mozzarella cheese and remove the pan from the heat. Stir everything for 30 seconds to ensure the cheese is fully incorporated. The heat from the sauce will melt the cheese.

In a small bowl, mix together the remaining 2 Tbsp of olive oil, the Panko, garlic, parsley, and thyme until a coarse crumbly mixture has formed.

Pour the cheese sauce over the eggplant in an even layer, scraping the pot clean. Sprinkle the Manchego cheese evenly over the top of the sauce then sprinkle it with the Panko mixture.

Bake for 25–30 minutes, until the eggplant is tender and the cheese is bubbling. If necessary, turn the broiler on to brown the top of the dish for 2–3 minutes before removing from the oven and serving.

This dish doesn't keep well and is best consumed the day it's made. Serve alongside grilled steaks with garlic aioli (page 115) or beans and rice (page 71), or braised chicken (page 103) for a delicious warm meal.

BASQUE-STYLE HAKE *with* SALSA VERDE
MERLUZA EN SALSA VERDE

In culinary terms, the Basque Region of Spain is a fascinating area. The city of San Sebastián in particular is one of the places where Spanish cuisine really came into its own. Influenced by its French neighbors, this city had one of the first Spanish cooking schools, and many well-known chefs have emerged from this region. If you can't find hake, cod, monkfish, or almost any meaty white fish with the skin on will be a great substitute.

To make the salsa, place all the ingredients in the blender and purée to form a thin green sauce.

In a large frying pan over medium heat, place all but ¼ cup of the salsa and bring it to a simmer. Allow it to simmer for 1–2 minutes to warm it through. Add the flour and stir to remove any lumps and to thicken slightly. Add half the fish stock and simmer for another minute.

Add the fish steaks, skin side down, and turn down the heat to low. Using a wooden spoon, gently move the steaks around a little to prevent them from sticking. Allow the sauce to simmer for another 2–3 minutes as the juices from the fish are released and incorporated.

Pour in the remaining fish stock and increase the heat back to medium. Bring the sauce to a strong simmer or a slow boil, stirring gently, and begin to spoon it over the top of the steaks. Continue in this way for 5–8 minutes, until the fish is just starting to flake away from the bone.

Remove from the heat and serve the fish with a spoonful of pan sauce over the top. Place the reserved sauce on the table for anyone who wants an extra dollop. The fish will keep in an airtight container in the fridge for 2–3 days, and the salsa will keep in a separate airtight container in the fridge for up to 2 weeks.

SERVES
FOUR

Salsa Verde
½ cup flat-leaf parsley leaves
2 cloves garlic
⅓ cup extra virgin olive oil
1 Tbsp Sherry vinegar
Sea salt
Hake
2 tsp all-purpose flour
½ cup fish stock
4 (each ½–¾ inch thick) hake steaks

In parsley season, or if the garden is overflowing with it, I'll make a big batch of salsa and freeze it in an ice cube tray. Once frozen, I'll transfer the cubes to a freezer bag for up to 6 months. It is perfect to add to eggs, soups, beans, and numerous other dishes for an extra pop of herbaceous flavor.

EMPANADILLAS

A tasty example of the Arab influence in Spain, these little meat pies originate from the Balearic Islands and Valencia. Empanadas, a larger version, are particularly popular in Galicia. The pies are now found all over Spain, in tapas bars as well as homes, with different regions offering their own twist on the recipe. Traditionally, these meat turnover–style pies are made with an olive oil pastry and stuffed with a tuna, pepper, and tomato filling. That said, now you can find them filled with everything from olives and pine nuts, to chorizo. So what differentiates them from pizza pockets? You'll rarely ever find them filled with cheese!

———————————

To make the dough, in a large mixing bowl, whisk together 2 cups of the flour, the salt, and baking powder until completely blended and lump-free. Make a well in the bottom and add the egg and olive oil. Whisk the egg and oil together slightly, and then, using a wooden spoon, slowly start to mix in the flour. Add the water and mix to form a soft dough.

Dust the counter with ½ cup of the remaining flour. Knead the dough gently, cover with a dry tea towel, and let rest at room temperature while you make the filling.

To make the filling, in a frying pan over medium heat, warm the olive oil and then sauté the onions for 3–4 minutes, until just turning golden. Sprinkle them with the salt and sauté for another minute. Deglaze the pan with the balsamic and continue to sauté, scraping any bits from the bottom of the pan, until almost all the liquid has been absorbed. Add the tomatoes and peppers and sauté for another 2–3 minutes, until the tomatoes are beginning to soften. Add the ginger and cumin, stir to fully combine, and then remove from the heat.

Makes about 16 small pies

Savory Olive Oil Pastry

3 cups all-purpose flour, divided

½ tsp sea salt

½ tsp baking powder

1 egg

½ cup Rosemary infused olive oil

¼ cup water

Filling

2 Tbsp extra virgin olive oil

1 small red onion, diced

1 tsp sea salt

2 Tbsp Grapefruit white balsamic vinegar

4 Roma tomatoes, diced

4 roasted red bell peppers, diced

1 tsp freshly grated ginger (or ½ tsp powdered ginger)

1 tsp ground cumin seeds

1 (5½ oz) can oil-packed tuna, rinsed and flaked

1 egg

Add the tuna to the vegetable mixture, folding it in gently to incorporate without breaking it up too much.

Preheat the oven to 350°F. Line a baking tray with parchment paper.

Cut the pastry dough in half and roll out the first half into a large rectangle about ¼ inch thick. Using a 5-inch round cookie cutter or a small bowl, cut out as many circles you're able. Gently pick up the leftover dough from around the circles and add it to the remaining dough. Spoon 2 Tbsp of the filling slightly off center onto each circle. Gently brush the outside of the circles with water, then holding the side of the circle with less filling on it, fold the pastry over to make a half-moon shape. Gently press the edges of the pastry together. Place it on the prepared baking tray and repeat with the remaining circles of dough. Repeat the process with the second piece of dough and the remaining filling.

In a measuring cup or a small bowl, whisk together the egg and a little bit of water. Brush the pastry with this egg wash.

Bake empanadillas for 30 minutes, until golden brown. Serve immediately.

These will keep in an airtight container in the fridge for up to 3 days, or can be frozen before baking for up to 3 months. If using from frozen, allow them to thaw completely before baking.

STEAMED MUSSELS
MEJILLONES AL VAPOR

Galicia is full of mussel farms, and in this northern corner of Spain, it's common to find them as a tapa, simply steamed with some onion, garlic-smoked paprika, and white wine. Of course, they're served in many other ways too—with salsa verde or a tomato and sherry sauce, and often stuffed and fried as commonly found in Madrid. Personally, I love to mix a few of the regional favorites together, creating a lovely sauce that is best sopped up with bread after the mussels are finished for a filling and delicious main course.

———————

Clean the mussels by rinsing them well, trimming off their beards, and scrubbing their shells. Discard any mussels that are not tightly closed or that have cracked shells.

In a large, heavy-bottomed saucepan over medium heat, sauté the onion and garlic in the olive oil. When the onions are just translucent, sprinkle them with the paprika, salt, and chili flakes, then sauté for another 2–3 minutes, until they're just turning golden and the spices are evenly spread throughout.

Dice the tomatoes and pepper and add them to the onions and garlic. Cook, stirring, for a few more minutes, until the tomatoes have broken down to make a thick sauce. Add the mussels, then pour in the sherry, stirring once to fully incorporate. Increase the temperature to medium-high and cover the pan. Allow the mussels to steam for about 5 minutes, or until they have all fully opened. Discard any that haven't opened by that point.

Spoon the mussels into serving dishes, top with a spoonful of sauce, and serve with lots of crusty bread on the side.

Mussels don't keep well and should be enjoyed as soon as they are made.

SERVES
FOUR
———

2-3 lb of mussels
(usually 3-4 dozen)

1 sweet white onion,
roughly chopped

4 cloves garlic, crushed,
in large pieces

¼ cup Rosemary infused olive oil

2 tsp smoked paprika

1 tsp sea salt

½ tsp chili flakes

2 tomatoes on the vine

1 yellow bell pepper

1 cup Manzanilla sherry

———

The first time I had mussels I was lucky enough to have them freshly caught and prepared at a friend's house. Rebekah grew up near the Bay of Fundy. Her trick to eating the shellfish was to use the shells as little tongs. She would quickly look through the dish to see if any shells were empty, then fish out that empty shell and use the ends like little pinchers to pry out the mussels from all the other shells.

ANDALUSIAN FISH FRY
PESCADO ANDALUZ

Although originally from Cádiz, this dish and method of frying fish are now one of the most common and popular ways of preparing fish in Spain. Andalusia is the home not only of some of the best fish in the country but also of olive oil, so it's not a big surprise that this crispy fried fish is perfectly golden, tender, and not greasy at all. The Grapefruit white balsamic vinegar tenderizes the fish, further ensuring that it is tasty and delicious.

Traditionally, a blend of small whiting fish, whole flounder, and snapper is used, but those can be hard to find in North America. The best substitute is the freshest trout, bass, rockfish, or porgy you can find. Whether you're using whole fish or fillets, do your best to purchase them cleaned, skinned, and headless.

SERVES
FOUR

3-4 lb (total weight) of headless fresh fish fillets (trout, bass, rockfish all work), skinned

¼ cup Grapefruit white balsamic vinegar

1 Tbsp sea salt, divided

Extra virgin olive oil for frying

1 cup all-purpose flour

1 cup cornmeal

Lemon wedges and Sherry vinegar for garnish (optional)

Rinse the fish well and pat dry with paper towels. Place fillets on a baking tray and drizzle each one with a few teaspoons of the balsamic and sprinkle with half the salt. Flip the fillets over and drizzle with the remaining vinegar and salt. Place in the fridge, uncovered, for 10–15 minutes.

In a deep-fryer or Dutch oven over medium-high heat, bring 1½ inches of olive oil to 350°F–375°F.

While the olive oil is heating up, mix together the flour and cornmeal in a shallow baking dish. Remove the fish from the fridge and dredge each fillet in the flour mixture.

Fry the fish for 3–4 minutes per side, one or two pieces at a time to avoid crowding the pan, turning the fish once it is golden brown on the outside. Allow the oil to come back up to temperature between batches.

Serve immediately with lemon wedges on the side and some Sherry vinegar (if using).

PAN-FRIED WHITE FISH in GRAPEFRUIT SAFFRON SAUCE

This delicious and beautiful dish is a speciality in Cádiz, where you'll find fish in almost every dish. When you're buying saffron, look for dark burgundy strands for the best flavor. It's a tricky ingredient—use too little and it's almost like it's not there at all and it feels like a waste of something very special, but use too much and it will be overpowering and bitter. However, the creamy complexity of the extra virgin olive oil and acidity of the Grapefruit white balsamic vinegar in this recipe not only complement the flavor profile of the saffron but also cut through its bitterness, so here I always err on the side of too much saffron rather than too little. The result? Magnificent.

———————————

Rinse the fish, pat it dry with a paper towel, and set aside.

In the bottom of a shallow 9- × 9-inch baking dish, whisk together the vinegar, 2 Tbsp of the olive oil, and the mustard. Place the fish in the baking dish and turn each piece to coat evenly. Remove the leaves from the sprigs of thyme and oregano and sprinkle them on top of the fish, along with 1 tsp of the salt and the pepper.

Cover with plastic wrap and place in the fridge for 30 minutes, or up to 2 hours, to marinate.

In a heavy-bottomed frying pan over medium heat, warm the remaining 2 Tbsp olive oil.

In a shallow dish, mix together the flour and cornstarch. Carefully remove the fish from the marinade and allow each piece to drain, reserving the marinade. Gently pat the fish dry with paper towel and dredge each piece through the flour to lightly coat, shaking off any excess.

Line a plate with paper towel.

Fry the fish in the warm oil for 3–4 minutes per side, until the flour is just turning golden brown. Remove the fish from the pan and set it on the prepared plate to drain.

SERVES
FOUR
———

4 (each ½ lb) pieces of meaty white fish (ling cod or halibut are lovely here)

¼ cup Grapefruit white balsamic vinegar

4 Tbsp extra virgin olive oil

2 tsp creamy Dijon mustard

2 sprigs thyme

2 sprigs oregano

1½ tsp sea salt

½ tsp cracked black pepper

¼ cup all-purpose flour

2 Tbsp cornstarch

½ tsp toasted cumin seeds

Generous pinch saffron

1 clove garlic

2 Roma tomatoes

1 small red onion

1 red bell pepper

1 yellow bell pepper

1 cup vegetable stock

Don't worry about the fish not being fully cooked, as it will finish cooking in the sauce.

Using a mortar and pestle, grind together the remaining ½ tsp salt, the cumin seeds, and saffron to a fine powder, then add the garlic clove and mash it all into a thick paste.

Finely chop the tomatoes, onion, and bell peppers.

In a Dutch oven or heavy-bottomed frying pan (you can always quickly wipe out the pan you fried the fish in), heat the remaining 2 Tbsp of olive oil. Gently stir in the saffron-garlic paste, then add the onion and peppers. Sauté for 1–2 minutes, until the onion is just translucent, then add the tomatoes and cook, stirring gently, for 5 minutes. Add the reserved marinade and cook for an additional 5–10 minutes, until the sauce has reduced and is a rich golden color. Stir in the fish stock, add the pieces of fish to the pan, and bring to a boil, spooning the sauce over the fish. Cook for another 5–10 minutes, until the sauce has reduced and the fish is fully cooked through.

Serve immediately, with the sauce spooned over the fish. I like to serve this with a side of Spanish rice or roasted vegetables.

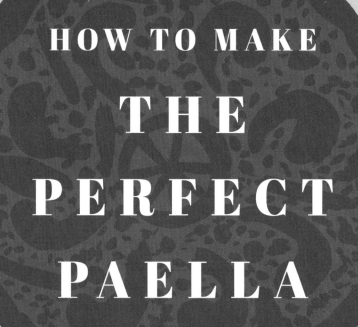

HOW TO MAKE

THE

PERFECT

PAELLA

You might be surprised to learn that paella is traditionally made with rabbit and snails. The snails have typically eaten rosemary bushes for most of their lives, so they're plump and very herbaceous in flavor. Originally cooked over an open wood fire in the rice fields in Valencia, this dish has now become a classic in tourist destinations and known throughout North America as a traditional Spanish food. It's not entirely accurate, but such is culinary life. The number of paella recipes out there, authentic or otherwise, is a little mind-boggling. The variations are endless: you'll find shrimp, scallop, and seaweed in some; quail and mushrooms, or lamb and red peppers, in others; and duck, olives, and sherry, as is traditional in Seville. You can also find paella made with black rice. (Check out Wikipaella for more amazing paella facts.)

The trick to delicious paella is the *socarrat*, the crisp rice on the bottom of the pan. Ensuring your pan is evenly heated and not stirred once the liquid is added ensures this will form and add character and complexity to the final dish.

While testing the paella recipes, my husband and I hosted numerous dinner parties—sometimes three in a week—because who can eat that much paella? We would crowd a group of hungry friends around a folding table in our driveway and they would enjoy tapas while I cooked the paella on the grill. My favorite part of serving up this dish was that because everything was prepped and ready to go, I was able to enjoy conversation and not feel stuck in the kitchen, so the cooking process was really fun. It's now my favorite food to make for friends.

SEAFOOD PAELLA

This version of paella is made with a mixture of shellfish and white fish, as is traditional in seaside communities. If you're a shellfish person, feel free to substitute more shellfish for the fish, and, of course, vice versa. (See page 98 for a meat-based paella.) A paella pan is the only way to go for the paella recipes.

———————————

Start by making a fire in a charcoal BBQ with 80–90 briquettes. While the grill is heating up, prepare all the ingredients.

Scrub the clams and mussels to get any bits of dirt off the shell, then trim the beards and rinse them well. Discard any clams or mussels that have broken shells or are not tightly closed. Set aside in a bowl.

Cut the cleaned squid in half and ensure that the beaks have been removed. Then slice them into 1-inch pieces and place them in a separate bowl.

Rinse the shrimp and remove the shells, if desired, leaving on the tails for ease of eating. Place them in a separate bowl.

Rinse and clean the fish, then cut it into large bite-size pieces. Place the pieces in the bowl with the squid. Put all the seafood in the fridge until you're ready to cook.

Place the stock in a large saucepan over medium heat and add the saffron threads, bring to a simmer, and then turn down the heat to low to keep the stock warm.

Finely chop the onion and crush the garlic, leaving the cloves in large pieces. Place them in a separate small bowl.

Chop the peppers and tomatoes, and place each in separate bowls as well.

When the fire is hot and the coals are white, place your paella pan on the grill and drizzle in the olive oil. Add the onions and garlic to the pan and sauté for 2–3

12 clams

12 mussels

6 small squid, cleaned

12 jumbo shrimp or
18 small shrimp

1 lb white fish, such
as cod, cleaned

6 cups warm fish stock

6-8 strands of saffron

1 small red onion

6 cloves garlic

2 red bell peppers

4 Roma tomatoes

¼ cup Rosemary infused olive oil

2 tsp sea salt

2 Tbsp Grapefruit white
balsamic vinegar

2 tsp sweet paprika

2½ cups short-grain rice

Curly parsley for garnish
(optional)

minutes, until tender. Sprinkle them with the 2 tsp salt, add the peppers, and continue to cook, stirring, for an additional 2–3 minutes.

Add the balsamic. Allow the onions to soak it all up and scrape up any bits sticking to the pan. Add the tomatoes and sprinkle with the paprika, continuing to stir until the tomatoes are soft and have broken down. If the pan is completely dry, add a little more olive oil. Add the rice, stirring well to ensure that it's well distributed and incorporated into the vegetables. Spread the rice around the paella pan in an even layer, and then place the pieces of fish and the squid evenly on top.

Gently pour 4 cups of the stock over the rice. It is very important from this point on that you don't stir the rice. Socarrat is the crispy golden rice that forms at the bottom of the dish, and it won't form if the rice is stirred.

Let the paella cook for 10–15 minutes, uncovered, until the rice is almost completely tender and only has a bit of crunch left and the pan is almost completely dry.

Nestle the clams and mussels evenly around the rice. If you're using jumbo shrimp with the shell on, add them now. If you're using small, shelled shrimp, wait to add them. Pour the remaining 2 cups of stock over the rice and cook for another 5 minutes, covering the grill with a lid to allow the steam to cook the clams and mussels. If you're using small, shelled shrimp, add them now. Check the rice to see if it's tender, adding a little more stock or water if it still has a crunch to it. If it's tender, cook it for an additional 2 minutes to ensure the socarrat is well formed. Remove the paella from the grill, cover with foil, and let sit for 5 minutes. Garnish with the parsley (if using) before serving. (See page 99 for an oven-cooking option. For this version, start with the onions and add the fish and squid to the paella pan before putting it in the oven to bake. Add the shellfish 5 minutes before the paella is finished to ensure the seafood doesn't overcook.)

Seafood paella doesn't keep well, so enjoy it the day it is made. With the seafood removed, the rice will keep for up to 3 days in an airtight container in the fridge.

CHICKEN and CHORIZO PAELLA

Although again not entirely traditional, this is my favorite blend of protein for a nonseafood paella. Using spicy chorizo, chicken drumsticks, and a mixture of bell peppers adds color and so much flavor without the need to gather a wide range of ingredients and ensures everything is well done by the end of the process. It's very common to add rosemary to the stock when making a meat-based paella, and incorporating the Rosemary infused olive oil here adds the earthiness needed without overpowering the other flavors. It will have your friends asking to take home the leftovers at the end of the evening!

Place the stock in a large saucepan over low heat. Add the saffron and allow to simmer gently to warm. When using the charcoal grill, warm stock is essential, or it will cool the flame too much and it won't cook properly.

Finely chop the onion, and crush and roughly chop the garlic. Place them in a bowl. Cut the bell peppers into 1-inch slices and chop the tomato. Place the bell pepper and tomatoes in separate piles on the cutting board or in separate bowls. Slice the chorizo into 1-inch pieces.

Place 120 charcoal briquettes in the bottom of a charcoal barbecue, light the grill, and wait for about 10 minutes for all of them to catch. If using a gas barbecue, preheat the grill to high.

Place the paella pan on the grill and drizzle in the olive oil. Add the chicken legs and, using a long set of tongs, turn the chicken so it browns evenly. There's no need for the chicken to cook fully; the skin just needs to sear and crisp.

Add the onions and garlic, and continue to sauté until the onions are starting to brown, 2–3 minutes, then add the chorizo and continue to cook, still turning the chicken and ensuring that everything is browning and cooking together.

SERVES
FOUR-SIX

6 cups warm chicken stock

8-10 strands of saffron

1 large red onion

6 cloves garlic

2 large bell peppers, variety of colors

2 large tomatoes

4 links fresh chorizo sausage

¼ cup Rosemary infused olive oil, plus some extra

8 chicken legs, skin on

¼ cup Sherry vinegar

2 Tbsp smoked paprika

2 cups paella or short-grain rice

Pour in the vinegar to deglaze the pan and scrape up onion bits from the bottom. Add the tomatoes, sprinkle with the paprika, and cook them until they're soft and the other vegetables are starting to cling like mud to the chicken. Add the peppers and sauté for 1–2 minutes.

Add the dry rice, and mix it in well. The rice will soak up the oil and become translucent. Toast it for 1–2 minutes, until no liquid remains in the pan, then arrange the chicken legs in a circle and evenly spread out the rice, chorizo, and vegetable mixture.

Slowly pour in the stock, starting from the outside, then pouring it over the chicken legs, washing the rice off them and ensuring that holes or pits don't form in the rice. Add just enough stock to come up to the top of the rivets where the handles attach to the paella pan.

Now walk away. Don't touch, stir, or rotate the pan at all for at least 15 minutes. The stock will boil and you'll hear the paella start to dry out as it sizzles.

This is the perfect time to join your guests in enjoying some tapas that you prepared earlier, or to clear up some dishes. This 15-minute break is one of the reasons this dish is a staple for all our summer dinner parties.

Once all the liquid has been absorbed, check the rice to see if it is tender. If it still has a bit of a crunch to it, add any remaining chicken stock to the pan and pop the lid on the barbecue for 2–3 minutes. After that, remove the lid and allow the rice to finish cooking. To check on the *socarrat*, gently poke the tongs into the rice and scrape the bottom of the paella pan. If some rice comes up in one chunk with a caramelized bottom, you know it's forming perfectly; if the rice scrapes easily and falls apart (as you would normally expect rice to do), leave the pan on the heat for another 3–5 minutes. Keep checking, gently, in different places around the pan until the rice is caramelized.

Remove from the heat and allow the paella to rest 5 minutes before serving.

Paella is best enjoyed fresh off the barbecue. But if you remove the chicken, the rice will keep for up to 3 days in an airtight container in the fridge and makes delicious lunches!

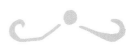

You can also make paella on the stovetop and in the oven. To do this, preheat your oven to 375°F and place the oven rack in the lowest position. Sear the chicken in the ¼ cup of olive oil in a large, heavy-bottomed frying pan over medium-high heat. Once browned, remove it from the pan. Add a touch more olive oil, then follow the directions for the onions, chorizo, and vegetables, including adding the rice. Scrape the rice and vegetable mixture into your paella pan and arrange the chicken in the rice mixture. Place the paella pan in the oven, gently and carefully pour in the stock, and then bake for 20 minutes. Check the rice to see if it's tender and if the bottom is caramelizing. Add more stock if needed, or remove from the oven if done. Let stand for 5 minutes, then serve and store as directed.

BRAISED CHICKEN
POLLO AL FRITADA

Fritada, similar to *sofrito*, is a mix of onions, peppers, and tomatoes that is used in many dishes from northeastern Spain. The Rosemary infused olive oil imbues an earthy flavor that makes this dish extra-special.

SERVES
FOUR

6 strips of bacon

4 Tbsp Rosemary infused olive oil, divided

4 chicken breasts, bone in and skin on

1 large red onion, roughly chopped

6 cloves garlic, crushed but kept whole

2 bell peppers, thinly sliced

Sea salt and cracked black pepper

2 Tbsp Sherry vinegar

1 (19 oz) can plum tomatoes

In a Dutch oven or large ovenproof frying pan over medium-high heat, fry the bacon until crispy. Remove it from the pan and set aside on a paper towel-covered plate.

Add 2 Tbsp of the olive oil to the bacon drippings, heat the pan on medium-high again, then add the chicken, skin side down. Allow the skin to brown and sear well, then remove from the pan and set aside.

Preheat the oven to 375°F.

Add the onions and garlic to the pan you used for the chicken. Over medium heat, sauté for 2–3 minutes, then add the peppers. Sprinkle everything with a little bit of sea salt to allow the onions and peppers to sweat. Add the vinegar, and stir well until all the liquid has been absorbed. Pour the juice from the can of tomatoes into the pan, then gently crush the tomatoes in your hand before adding them to the pan. Stirring constantly, increase the heat slightly and allow the mixture to come to a low boil. Stir for another minute, then remove from the heat.

Roughly chop the bacon and stir it into the sauce. Nestle the chicken breasts into the tomato pepper mixture, skin side up, drizzle the chicken with the remaining olive oil, and sprinkle with a little salt and pepper.

Bake, covered, for 30 minutes, until the chicken is no longer pink inside, the juices run clear, and the internal temperature of the chicken has reached 165°F.

Serve straight from the baking dish, with a spoonful of *fritada* on the side.

You can store this in an airtight container in the fridge for up to 5 days.

CHICKEN, RICE, and ROASTED RED PEPPERS

The fun part about this dish is that the chicken is cooked right in the rice, so the drippings turn into the stock, instantly making this superflavorful with little effort. The tricky part is taking the browned and beautiful chicken out of the pan when it's still piping hot. Often I'll carve the meat in the pan, then discard the carcass and spoon the rice onto our plates. The Rosemary infused olive oil combined with the Sherry vinegar are perfect in this dish. They draw together the subtle sweetness of the saffron and the richness of the peppers, ensuring that every bite of the rice is delicious.

———————————

Preheat the oven to 375°F.

In a frying pan over medium-high heat, sauté the onions and garlic in 2 Tbsp of the oil for 2–3 minutes, until the onions are just translucent. Sprinkle them with 1 tsp of the salt and sauté for another minute or two. Pour in the vinegar and continue to cook, stirring, for 5–8 minutes, until the onions are soft and golden brown. Scrape the onions into a blender and purée until completely smooth. Pour the mixture into a 9- × 13-inch roasting pan.

Pat the chicken dry, rub it all over with about 2 Tbsp of olive oil, and place it on top of the onion mixture in the roasting pan. Drizzle the remaining olive oil over the chicken, then sprinkle evenly with the remaining salt. Sprinkle the rice around the chicken into the pan and then slowly add the chicken stock, allowing it to flow in and around the rice. Sprinkle the saffron around the rice, mixing it gently to incorporate the onion sauce into the rice mixture as well. Slice the roasted red peppers in half and then nestle them around the chicken.

SERVES
FOUR · SIX
———

2 sweet white onions, finely chopped

4 cloves garlic, finely chopped

½ cup Rosemary infused olive oil, divided

2 tsp sea salt, divided

¼ cup Sherry vinegar

1 (4-5 lb) roasting chicken

2 cups short-grain rice

1½ cups chicken stock

6-8 strands of saffron

4 roasted red bell peppers (store-bought are fine)

Bake, covered with foil, for 30 minutes, then uncover and bake for another 20 minutes, until the rice is tender and the chicken has reached an internal temperature of 165°F.

If the rice is still a little dry or the liquid has evaporated fully, add a few more tablespoons of stock or water. The amount of stock the chicken produces will differ slightly based on the size and kind of chicken. I always find organic grass-fed chickens are the plumpest and juiciest, although everyday roasting hens are tasty too.

Serve by carving the chicken in the pan and scooping it up with the rice onto plates, or remove the chicken and carve it as you normally would, then scrape the rice into a serving dish to serve alongside.

Leftovers will keep for up to 3 days in an airtight container in the fridge.

ROASTED PORK BELLY with APPLES and PEARS
PANZA DE CERDO CON MANZANAS DE ASTURIAS

Asturias is the land of pork in Spain. The pigs are fattened on wild acorns, and sometimes chestnuts, in the fields, creating the most incredibly flavored ham. Asturias is also the land of apples—which makes sense, given that pork and apples are a match made in heaven. Often pork is now raised for its lean meat, so sometimes it's quite flavorless, because the fat is what adds so much flavor. In this dish the pork belly is rippled with flavorful fat and tender meat, the apples and pears are sweet, soft, and saucy, and the Rosemary infused olive oil-doused crackling is crispy. This is a fall favorite in our house and often lands on the Thanksgiving table along with the turkey and fixings.

SERVES
FOUR-SIX

2 large Granny Smith apples

2 large Bartlett pears

1 (3-4 lb) piece of pork belly, with the rind on

4 Tbsp Rosemary infused olive oil, divided

1 Tbsp + 1 tsp sea salt

½ cup apple cider

Preheat the oven to 450°F.

Peel, core, and slice the apples and pears and place them in an even layer on the bottom of a 9- × 13-inch roasting pan.

Wash the pork belly and pat it dry with paper towel. Place it rind side down on a cutting board, drizzle 2 Tbsp of the olive oil over the surface, and sprinkle with 1 tsp of the salt. Gently flip over the pork belly. Carefully score the rind in a crisscross manner, cutting about ¼ inch deep and being careful not to slice all the way through. Pat it dry with paper towel, drizzle with the remaining olive oil, and rub in the remaining 1 Tbsp of salt until it has been absorbed.

Place the pork belly rind side up on top of the layer of apples and pears in the roasting pan.

Bake, uncovered, for 15–20 minutes, until the rind has seared, has started to puff up a bit, and is turning golden brown.

Turn down the oven temperature to 375°F and gently pour the cider into a corner of the pan, without pouring any over the top of the rind.

Bake for another 60 minutes, and then check to see if the belly is tender, the apples and pears are soft, and the crackling is crisp and browned. If the crackling isn't quite done, turn on the broiler for a few minutes, watching it carefully to finish it.

Remove the pan from the oven and let sit for 5 minutes, uncovered, before serving. If you cover it, the cracking will moisten from the condensation. Transfer the pork belly to a serving board and scrape the fruit sauce into a serving bowl. Slice the pork into strips and serve with a dollop of the sauce on the side.

The belly will keep in an airtight container in the fridge for up to 5 days, although it's definitely best served the day it's made. The sauce should be kept in a jar or airtight bowl in the fridge and will keep for up to 2 weeks.

MIGAS

Comfort food in every form, *migas* was created by shepherds in the mountains of northern Spain. Originally, it was made with stale bread, rabbit, and sometimes chorizo. My favorite way to eat this is for breakfast, with bacon, chorizo, and a fried egg on top. Here, the Rosemary infused olive oil brings everything together and the Sherry vinegar adds an unmistakable brightness.

Tear the bread into ½-inch cubes and place in a mixing bowl. Warm the stock and vinegar in a small saucepan over medium-low heat, then whisk in the paprika. Pour this over the bread, stir to combine, then cover with plastic wrap. Let sit at room temperature for 1 hour, or overnight in the fridge, so the bread can soak up the liquid and flavors.

Warm 2 Tbsp of the olive oil in a large frying pan over medium heat. Sauté the onion and garlic for 2–3 minutes.

Cut the chorizo into bite-size pieces, and add them and the pork belly to the pan. Cook, stirring gently, for about 5 minutes, until the pork belly is just starting to brown and the chorizo is seared evenly all over. Season to taste with salt and pepper and cook for another 2–3 minutes.

Increase the heat to high and add the soaked bread. Fry the bread, breaking it up into smaller chunks and allowing it to crisp up and brown, about 15 minutes. The pieces will be like croutons—crunchy and golden on the outside and soft on the inside.

Remove from the heat and divide the mixture evenly between two warm serving plates.

Place the remaining 2 Tbsp of olive oil in the frying pan and fry the eggs. Place the eggs on top of the *migas* and serve immediately. Garnish with a sprig of rosemary and a dusting of paprika. These don't store well, so eat them as soon as you've cooked them.

SERVES
TWO

4 slices of bread, crusts on

¾ cup chicken or veggie stock

2 Tbsp Sherry vinegar

2 tsp sweet paprika

4 Tbsp Rosemary infused olive oil

1 red onion, finely chopped

4 cloves garlic, finely chopped

2 links of chorizo

½ cup chopped pork belly, or 4 slices of thick-cut bacon

Sea salt and cracked black pepper

2 eggs

The trick to this dish really is the bread. Buy the best you can find and this is sure to be a success. Sourdough is my favorite, although marble rye is a lovely change and adds so much flavor. Feel free to mix it up and use a few types of bread together if you like.

CARAMELIZED PORK MEDALLIONS
CERDO CON LECHE Y CARAMELO

When talking about caramel, the first thing that comes to mind is ice cream or Christmas, definitely not pork. This dish from the mountains of the Basque Region changed that for me.

Be warned that the milk does tend to curdle during the cooking process. This is totally normal, although personally I find it a bit unappetizing, so after the pork has cooked and before serving, I blend the sauce and pour it through a strainer to get rid of any lumps. If you're happy with it being a little more rustic, feel free to skip this step. Rosemary, citrus, and caramel are a favorite combination in general, and in this dish they will have guests wanting more.

———————————

Slice the pork tenderloin into 2-inch-thick medallions. Rub them all with salt and pepper.

In a large frying pan over medium heat, warm the olive oil and sear the medallions, in batches as to not overcrowd the pan, well on all sides. Don't rush this step.

Remove the tenderloin from the pan and set it aside. Pour the balsamic into the pan, still over medium heat, and deglaze it, scraping up any bits from the bottom. Remove the pan from the heat and set aside. You'll use it again, so don't clean it or put it away.

In a medium-size saucepan over medium heat, stir the sugar into the water and bring to a boil, stirring constantly. As soon as the caramel starts to bubble, stop stirring. Allow it to gently boil until it turns golden brown and the aroma of cooking caramel fills the kitchen. Pour in the cream and, using a wooden spoon, stir it in quickly. It will bubble up— that's OK. Stir constantly until the cream is fully incorporated and then remove the pan from the heat. Add the salt, and then pour in the milk and whisk to fully incorporate.

SERVES

FOUR

———

2 pork tenderloins

Sea salt and cracked black pepper

¼ cup Rosemary infused olive oil

2 Tbsp Grapefruit white balsamic vinegar

½ cup granulated sugar

¼ cup water

1 cup whipping (35%) cream

1 tsp sea salt

2 cups 2% milk

1 tsp pink peppercorns

1 orange or grapefruit

Place the frying pan back on medium-low heat. Nestle the medallions into the pan so they all fit snugly (some overlap is OK but try to minimize it). Pour in the caramel mixture and then sprinkle the peppercorns over the top. Slice (don't grate!) the peel off the orange or grapefruit and nestle it into the pan. Bring to a low boil, then turn down the heat to medium-low, half-cover the pan, and simmer for 30–45 minutes, until the tenderloin medallions are fully cooked through and have an internal temperature of 165°F.

To serve, place the tenderloin medallions in a shallow serving dish. Remove the peel and pour the contents of the pan into a blender to blend until fully combined. Pour the resulting sauce through a fine mesh strainer, or a strainer lined with a layer of cheesecloth, to remove any lumps. Pour the strained sauce over the medallions, reserving some in a gravy boat for extra-saucy goodness.

Store the pork in the sauce in an airtight container for up to 4 days.

GRILLED BEEF STEAKS with GARLIC AIOLI
FILETE DE BUEY A LA BRASA CON ALIOLI DE AJO

There is something so simple and classic about a steak grilled in olive oil. *Churrasquerías*, which are similar to steakhouses, are very common, especially in the Basque Region where they originated. Everything is cooked over a wood fire, and they often only serve meat (yes, meat and nothing else). The tradition has traveled to South America, and these restaurants are now staples in Brazilian and Argentinian culture. Many of the *churrasquerías* in northern Spain are actually owned by South American emigrants.

In this recipe, the creamy garlic aioli complements the flavor of the tender beef so well. Since there are so few ingredients, using the best ingredients you can find is essential, of course. In Spain, the steaks used are well aged from specially fattened cows, although here a beautiful thick-cut T-bone or rib eye will do the trick.

SERVES
FOUR

Aioli
2 egg yolks, at room temperature
1 tsp Sherry vinegar
2 cloves garlic
½ tsp sea salt
1 cup extra virgin olive oil

Meat
4 thick-cut (each ¾-inch thick and about 12 oz) steaks
⅓ cup extra virgin olive oil, divided, plus extra for the grill
Sea salt and cracked black pepper

Of course, these are best done over an open wood fire or charcoal grill. Gas barbecues also work, though, as does panfrying. Heat a few tablespoons of olive oil in a frying pan over medium-high heat and add the meat. Ensure it sears well by pressing down on it with a spatula. Flip the steak a few times for about 10 minutes until cooked to the desired color.

To make the aioli, place the egg yolks in a large bowl and whisk in the vinegar.

Using a mortar and pestle, mash the garlic and the salt together to form a thick paste, ensuring the garlic is totally pulverized and no small chunks are left. Scrape the paste into the egg yolks and whisk to fully combine.

Slowly drizzle in the olive oil, a few drops at a time, while whisking constantly to ensure the oil emulsifies evenly into the yolks. Increase the speed at which you're adding the oil until it reaches a fine drizzle. Continue to whisk and drizzle until the mixture is light, fluffy, and thickened. Set in the fridge until ready to use.

The aioli will keep in an airtight container in the fridge for up to 1 week.

To prepare the steaks, pat them dry and trim off any excess outer fat. Drizzle each of the steaks with 2 tsp of the olive oil and sprinkle generously with salt and pepper. Using your fingers, rub in the salt, pepper, and olive oil, then flip the steaks over and repeat the entire process on the other side. Let the steaks rest for a few minutes while the grill heats up.

Light a grill and wait until the coals are glowing and white, or the temperature reaches at least 400°F. Grease the grill well with olive oil, then place the steaks on top. Cover and let cook for 3–4 minutes, until well seared, then flip them and sear the other side for 3–4 minutes.

Flip the steaks again, and move them to a cooler part of the grill. Cook for 5 more minutes for rare, 8 more minutes for medium, and 10–15 more minutes for a well-done steak, flipping a few more times.

Remove the steaks from the grill and let rest on a cutting board for 5 minutes to finish cooking and allow the juices to set.

Serve with a dollop of aioli on the side. Keep leftover steak in an airtight container in the fridge for up to 1 week or in the freezer for up to 3 months.

POMEGRANATE PORK ROAST

This simple pork roast is as tender as it is sweet. The Grapefruit white balsamic vinegar makes for a lovely, bright, and citrusy glaze and the natural sugars in the vinegar help caramelize and thicken the sauce.

SERVES
SIX

2 cups pomegranate juice

½ cup Grapefruit white balsamic vinegar

3 sprigs thyme

10 black peppercorns

1 bay leaf

1 large red onion

2-3 lb boneless pork roast (loin is best)

2 tsp sea salt

1 tsp cumin seeds

½ tsp coriander seeds

3 Tbsp Rosemary infused olive oil

In a saucepan over medium heat, place the pomegranate juice, balsamic, thyme, peppercorns, and bay leaf. Bring to a simmer and reduce volume reduce by half. Remove the herbs and peppercorns. You should have just over 1 cup of sauce.

While the sauce is simmering, slice the onion into rounds and place them in a 7- × 11-inch roasting pan. Set aside.

Preheat the oven to 375°F.

Rinse the pork roast and pat it dry with some paper towel. Using a small mortar and pestle, grind together the sea salt, cumin seeds, and coriander seeds. Rub the roast all over with the olive oil, and then gently pat the salt and spice mixture all over it.

Place the roast fat side up in the roasting pan on top of the bed of onions. Pour the pomegranate reduction over the top and roast, covered with foil, for 1 hour. Check the roast after 40 minutes to see how much liquid is in the pan. If there is plenty, spoon some over the top of the roast to allow it to baste a little. (In the unlikely event that the pan is dry, add a couple of tablespoons of water or stock.) After 1 hour, check the internal temperature of the roast. It should be close to 140°F. Turn on the broiler, remove the foil from the pan, and broil until the top of the roast is golden, 2–3 minutes. Remove from the oven, cover with foil, and let rest at least 10 minutes. Check the internal temperature, as it will continue to increase. It should reach 165°F.

Carve the roast and serve with the drippings on the side. You can store leftover meat and sauce in separate airtight containers in the fridge for up to 1 week.

The Moors called the Balearic Islands home for several centuries, and many local dishes in Spain reflect a Moorish influence, which typically combines fruit into meat dishes.

COCKTAILS

GIN TONIC

The Spanish version of this classic English cocktail, which omits the ampersand in its name, is considered the national cocktail of Spain and first became popular in the Basque Region. Served in a balloon or large wine glass to allow the botanical aroma of the gin to come forward, it's always piled high with ice cubes (not crushed ice) to allow for slow melting, which allows more aroma to be released. Garnishes abound: fresh herbs and citrus peels, cucumber and olives, even caper berries can be found in the glass. This could possibly be the perfect version of a classic cocktail.

SERVES

ONE

2 oz gin of choice

4 oz premium tonic water

1 tsp Grapefruit white balsamic vinegar

1 sprig rosemary

Fill a large wine glass with as many ice cubes as you can pile in—8 to 10 cubes is not considered excessive.

Pour the gin over the ice cubes, top with the tonic and balsamic, and stir once to combine.

Garnish with rosemary (and any other seasonal garnish desired).

When choosing a tonic water, look for a good-quality brand. If you're using a delicious premium gin, remember it is actually only a small portion of the beverage. The tonic is more than half the drink, so using a tasty artisan tonic is the best way to ensure every sip of your drink is delicious. If good tonic isn't to be found, a dry hard cider is a great substitute.

SPANISH NEGRONI

The classic negroni is not something to be trifled with. Bitter yet sweet, floral yet intensely flavorful, it is extremely well balanced. That said, adding a bit of Amontillado sherry for a drier flavor, or Oloroso sherry for a slightly sweeter and richer flavor, pulls all the pieces together for a delicious twist on this classic.

———————————

Place all the liquid ingredients in a cocktail shaker filled with ice cubes and stir.

Strain into a tumbler-style glass and serve with a large ice cube.

Garnish with a twist of orange and an olive.

SERVES
ONE

¾ oz gin

¾ oz medium-dry sherry

¾ oz Campari

¾ oz sweet Vermouth

Splash of Grapefruit white balsamic vinegar

Twist of orange and an olive to garnish

VOODOO TATTOO

One of my favorites from Josh Boudreau of Veneto Tapa Lounge, this tasty concoction is creamy and sweet and best enjoyed in front of a fire on a chilly evening. The yellow Chartreuse has a mild, sweet, yet herbaceous aroma and complements the richness of the sherry paired with the sweetness of the maraschino liqueur. The citrus brightens each sip and allows each flavor to shine.

————————————

Fill a tumbler-style glass with crushed ice.

Place all the ingredients in an ice cube-filled cocktail shaker, and stir to combine.

Empty the glass and strain in the contents of the cocktail shaker.

Serve with a few ice cubes and add a twist of orange for garnish.

1 oz Spanish brandy
1 oz cream sherry
½ oz yellow Chartreuse
½ oz maraschino liqueur
½ oz fresh lime juice
Twist of orange for garnish

SANGRIA

My version of this well-known Spanish wine punch isn't exactly traditional, although it sure is tasty! Found in all the tourist places in Spain, and on almost every restaurant menu in North America too, sangria is the perfect summer beverage to enjoy on a sunny patio with lots of great company. The Grapefruit white balsamic vinegar adds such a delicious bright quality to the drink and allows you to enjoy so many other fruits without needing to add a bunch of citrus.

Slice the orange into rounds, slice the apple and the peach into wedges, and place them all in a shallow 9- × 9-inch baking dish. Slice the strawberries in half, add them to the baking dish, and top with the blackberries.

Drizzle the fruit with the rum and the balsamic. Cover the dish with plastic wrap, place in the fridge, and allow the fruit to macerate for at least 1 hour, or up to overnight.

When ready to serve, carefully pour the juice and the fruit into a large pitcher. Top with wine and stir to combine.

Serve in glasses with a few ice cubes topped up with some soda water.

This is best enjoyed the day it is made, although it will keep overnight in the fridge once assembled if desired.

SERVES
FOUR

---

1 orange

1 apple

1 peach

4–6 large strawberries

4–6 large blackberries

½ cup rum or brandy

¼ cup Grapefruit white balsamic vinegar

1 bottle of fruity red wine

2 cups soda water

MIND OVER MATTER

This recipe is my adaption of one of the most popular cocktails at a favorite local cocktail lounge in Victoria. Brian Newham created the original version of this delicious beverage by combining the complexity of sweet cream sherry with a bright and flavorful bourbon and balancing it all with the richness of fresh plum, vanilla, and ever-bright Sherry vinegar. Peychaud's bitters, which were created by a Creole apothecary from Haiti who settled in New Orleans in 1795 and were originally distributed by the Sazerac Company, come from the root of the gentian flower and are sweeter, more floral, and lighter than Angostura bitters.

SERVES
ONE

½ ripe red plum

1 tsp pure vanilla extract

1 tsp Sherry vinegar

1 ½ oz Maker's Mark bourbon

¾ oz cream sherry

2 dashes Peychaud's bitters

Slice the plum half and place it in a cocktail shaker. Add the vanilla and Sherry vinegar and muddle to extract the plum juices.

Top with ice cubes and add the remaining ingredients. Stir, then pour through a strainer into a small glass. Serve with a large round ice cube.

EVERYTHING IS GOING to BE ALL RIGHT

This is very true. When the world around us seems to be falling apart, having hope and faith that "everything is going to be all right" is needed—and sometimes a sip of this delicious drink, created by Simon Ogden of Veneto Tapa Lounge, is what we need to take a moment and reflect, or just think about all delicious layered flavors in this cocktail and how every sip is equally delicious yet somehow totally unique. Your first sip when the cocktail is bright and cold will bring forward the cinnamon and nutmeg; as the cocktail warms a little, the notes of ginger, cardamom, and fennel become more apparent. A Fino sherry, which is very dry, complements the effervescent and sweeter cava (a Spanish sparkling wine), ensuring that everything is increasingly OK with every sip.

Fill a fluted glass with ice to chill for a few minutes.

Pour the sherry and chai syrup into a cocktail shaker and stir with ice cubes to chill.

Discard the ice in the flute and strain the sherry and chai mixture into the glass. Top the glass with cava, drop in the cherry, and serve.

SERVES
ONE

1 oz Fino sherry
¾ oz chai syrup
Cava to top up your glass
Cherry for garnish

Fino sherry, the driest sherry, is created and fermented with a layer of yeast on top of the grape juice to prevent contact with the air. This creates a very dry, saline, and herbaceous, almost yeast-like flavor profile.

THE DOUGIE

Sometimes you need a little liquid courage to get your dancing shoes on, and other times you're looking for a tasty drink to keep you grounded. Ken Gifford of Wolf in the Fog, the creator of this deliciously warm, rich, and nutty concoction, knows how to warm the heart and the toes, so no matter your style, this cocktail is sure to please.

SERVES
ONE

1½ oz blended Scotch whisky

1½ oz cream sherry

¼ oz Bénédictine

2 dashes Fee Brothers Black Walnut bitters

Twist of orange to garnish

Fill a cocktail glass of your choice with crushed ice.

Blend all the ingredients in a cocktail shaker filled with ice cubes.

Empty the prepared glass, add 2–3 ice cubes, and strain in the contents of the shaker.

Serve with a twist of orange.

EL JEFE

This aptly named citrus-forward cocktail is not easily forgotten. It is the perfect way to start an evening and should be enjoyed often with friends. Josh Boudreau of Veneto Tapa Lounge in Victoria favors an Oloroso sherry, a medium-dry sherry that often has tasting notes of dried fruit and rich spices. Thanks to the pairing of this sherry with the tang of the lemon and grapefruit and the effervescent sweetness of the cava, it's no wonder this cocktail is "the boss."

———————————

Put the sherry, Limoncello, and balsamic in a fluted glass. Top with cava and serve with a twist of lime or lemon.

SERVES
ONE

1 oz Oloroso sherry

¾ oz Limoncello

Dash of Grapefruit white balsamic vinegar

Cava to fill the glass

Twist of lime or lemon for garnish

BAMBOO COCKTAIL

In many ways a sherry martini, this classic was created by Louis Eppinger at the Grand Hotel in Yokoama, Japan, around 1890 for visiting dignitaries. Incorporating two kinds of bitters into this cocktail creates a very citrus-forward aromatic complement to the sherry and dry vermouth.

―――――――――

Fill a coupe or martini-style glass with ice cubes.

Place all the ingredients in an ice cube-filled cocktail shaker and stir to combine.

Empty out your glass of choice and strain the contents of the cocktail shaker into it.

Garnish with a twist of lemon.

SERVES
ONE

1½ oz dry Amontillado sherry
1½ oz Noilly Prat dry vermouth
2 dashes orange bitters
1 dash Angostura bitters
Lemon twist for garnish

―――――――――

Ensure your vermouth is fresh. Although most assume that vermouth is a stable spirit that will last forever, it is actually a fortified wine with a relatively short shelf life. During Prohibition, bartenders left North America for Europe and beyond, taking their knowledge and expertise with them. Not surprisingly, when Prohibition ended, all the bottles were still in many of the lounges in America and new bartenders started making cocktails with them. This is one of the reasons why the volume of vermouth in a classic North American martini has decreased steadily since Prohibition ended—the vermouth used was oxidized and old, so it didn't have the same impact, shall we say, as fresh.

HOT CHOCOLATE and CHURROS

This delicious hot chocolate is served alongside *churros* for dunking, and is often served for breakfast in Spain. Adding a touch of cornstarch to the mix thickens the chocolate just enough for it to fully coat the churro. Any leftovers can be added to a fresh cup of coffee for an impromptu mocha. The mild extra virgin olive oil ensures a silky-smooth texture and adds a lovely finish to the chocolate. Arbequina and Hojiblanca are my favorite varietals for frying the churros.

———————————

Place the chocolate in a medium-size saucepan.

In a small dish, mix together the cornstarch and cinnamon, then mix in the olive oil to form a smooth paste. If there are still a few lumps, add a few tablespoons of the milk to thin it out a bit. Add the olive oil mixture, milk, and sugar to the pot. Stir to combine and remove any lumps.

Place the pot over medium-high heat and bring just to a boil, stirring constantly to prevent any new lumps from forming. Allow it to boil for 1 minute, then remove from the heat. Pour into serving mugs and serve alongside churros.

CHURROS

In a small saucepan over medium-high heat, bring the water, olive oil, and salt to a boil. As soon as it reaches boiling point, turn down the heat to the lowest setting. Add the flour all at once and stir vigorously to fully incorporate and prevent any lumps from forming. The dough will pull away from the side of the pot and form a ball.

Let the dough cool enough to handle, then transfer it to a pastry bag fitted with a large fluted tip.

Heat at least 1 inch of olive oil in the bottom of a large heavy-bottomed saucepan or frying pan over medium-high heat to 350°F–375°F. Pipe 4–6-inch lengths of dough

SERVES
FOUR
————

Hot Chocolate
6 oz bittersweet chocolate, roughly chopped
3 tsp cornstarch
¼ tsp ground cinnamon
1 Tbsp mild extra virgin olive oil
4 cups whole (3.25%) milk
¼ cup granulated sugar
Churros
Makes six to eight churros
1 cup water
1 Tbsp extra virgin olive oil
¼ tsp sea salt
1 cup all-purpose flour
Extra virgin olive oil for frying
Granulated sugar for garnish

(three or four at a time, to avoid overcrowding the pan) into the hot oil, being careful not to splash the olive oil when the end of the churro drops into it. Fry for 2–3 minutes until golden brown, turning once. Give the oil a minute or two to reheat. Repeat with the remaining dough. Dust freshly cooked churros with sugar and serve immediately.

Churros don't keep well and should be consumed warm, fresh from the pan.

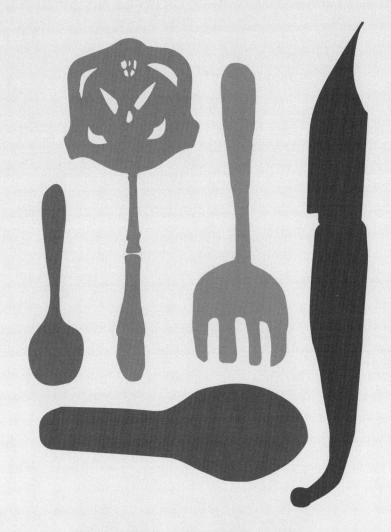

MENUS

TAPAS NIGHT

Tomato Bread (page 13)

Marinated Olives (page 39)

Grilled Garlic Prawns with Chili (page 33)

Croquettes (page 16)

Patatas Bravas (page 31)

Homemade Chorizo Cooked in Cider with Honey (page 23)

Sherry-Roasted Wild Mushrooms (page 29)

Gin Tonic (page 123)

AN EVENING WITH PAELLA

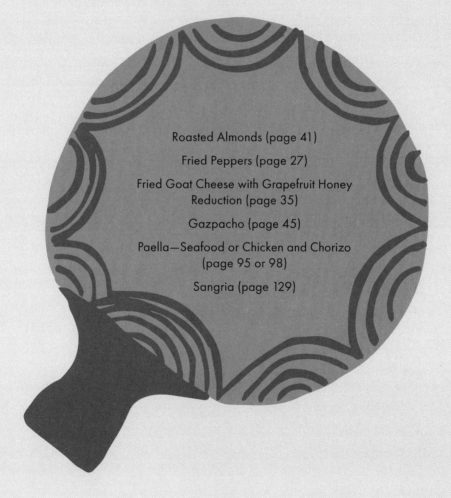

Roasted Almonds (page 41)

Fried Peppers (page 27)

Fried Goat Cheese with Grapefruit Honey
Reduction (page 35)

Gazpacho (page 45)

Paella—Seafood or Chicken and Chorizo
(page 95 or 98)

Sangria (page 129)

FISH FAVORITES

Endive and Citrus Two-Bite
Salad Cups (page 67)

Grilled Onions with
Romesco Sauce (page 37)

Steamed Mussels (page 85)

Andalusian Fish Fry (page 87)

El Jefe (page 135)

SIMPLE COZY ELEGANCE

Roasted Tomato Salad (page 65)

Spanish Stew (page 54)

Voodoo Tattoo (page 127)

Hot Chocolate and
Churros (page 139)

METRIC CONVERSIONS CHART

VOLUME	
⅛ tsp	0.5 mL
¼ tsp	1 mL
½ tsp	2.5 mL
¾ tsp	4 mL
1 tsp	5 mL
1½ tsp	7.5 mL
2 tsp	10 mL
1 Tbsp	15 mL
4 tsp	20 mL
2 Tbsp	30 mL
3 Tbsp	45 mL
¼ cup/4 Tbsp	60 mL
5 Tbsp	75 mL
⅓ cup	80 mL
½ cup	125 mL
⅔ cup	160 mL
¾ cup	185 mL
1 cup	250 mL

VOLUME	
1¼ cups	310 mL
1½ cups	375 mL
1¾ cups	435 mL
2 cups/1 pint	500 mL
2¼ cups	560 mL
2½ cups	625 mL
3 cups	750 mL
3½ cups	875 mL
4 cups/1 quart	1 L
4½ cups	1.125 L
5 cups	1.25 L
5½ cups	1.375 L
6 cups	1.5 L
6½ cups	1.625 L
7 cups	1.75 L
8 cups	2 L
12 cups	3 L

VOLUME	
¼ fl oz	7.5 mL
½ fl oz	15 mL
¾ fl oz	22 mL
1 fl oz	30 mL
1½ fl oz	45 mL
2 fl oz	60 mL
3 fl oz	90 mL
4 fl oz	125 mL
5 fl oz	160 mL
6 fl oz	185 mL
8 fl oz	250 mL
24 fl oz	750 mL

WEIGHT	
1 oz	30 g
2 oz	60 g
3 oz	90 g
¼ lb/4 oz	125 g
5 oz	150 g
6 oz	175 g
½ lb/8 oz	250 g
9 oz	270 g
10 oz	300 g
¾ lb/12 oz	375 g
14 oz	400 g
1 lb	500 g
1½ lb	750 g
2 lb	1 kg
2½ lb	1.25 kg
3 lb	1.5 kg
4 lb	1.8 kg
5 lb	2.3 kg
5½ lb	2.5 kg
6 lb	2.7 kg

LENGTH	
⅛ inch	3 mm
¼ inch	6 mm
⅜ inch	9 mm
½ inch	1.25 cm
¾ inch	2 cm
1 inch	2.5 cm
1½ inches	4 cm
2 inches	5 cm
3 inches	8 cm
4 inches	10 cm
4½ inches	11 cm
5 inches	12 cm
6 inches	15 cm
7 inches	18 cm
8 inches	20 cm
8½ inches	22 cm
9 inches	23 cm
10 inches	25 cm
11 inches	28 cm
12 inches	30 cm

OVEN TEMPERATURE	
40°F	5°C
120°F	49°C
125°F	51°C
130°F	54°C
135°F	57°C
140°F	60°C
145°F	63°C
150°F	66°C
155°F	68°C
160°F	71°C
165°F	74°C
170°F	77°C
180°F	82°C
200°F	95°C
225°F	107°C
250°F	120°C
275°F	140°C
300°F	150°C
325°F	160°C
350°F	180°C
375°F	190°C
400°F	200°C
425°F	220°C
450°F	230°C
475°F	240°C
500°F	260°C

CAN SIZES	
4 oz	114 mL
14 oz	398 mL
19 oz	540 mL
28 oz	796 mL

ACKNOWLEDGMENTS

Thank you to the friends, loved ones, and faithful customers who have inspired these recipes and encouraged me on this journey. As my food-nerdiness evolves and my love for olive oil and vinegar deepens, I continue to be amazed at all the wonderful people in my life who lift me up and bring it all together.

Steve, even though this is supposed to be a note of appreciation, it's me, so that means it should start with an apology. I'm sorry for inflicting nine renditions of paella upon you, and filling our driveway with friends three times a week so they could critique these recipes. I'm sorry I continued to make you count the briquettes you added to the barbecue on every occasion or recipe attempt. I'm sorry for waking you up before daybreak so I could catch a ferry to Salt Spring for photo shoots on your days off, or sending you on late-night grocery runs when you had to work early in the morning, and for those other days when I needed you to take Cedrik for a walk so I could focus and write. After all is said and done, it was pretty fun, wasn't it? You put all the pieces together and you make this dream a reality. Thank you for supporting my vision and walking beside me every step of the way.

Danielle, you are the best partner in crime, and these recipes would be nothing without your exceptional talent and creative genius. These images come alive and jump off the page. Working with you is such a privilege, not to mention how much I love the chance to cook for your family, our late-night talks and Pinterest brainstorming sessions, and treasure the cozy nights in your beautiful cottage. I look forward to our days together and can't wait to see what comes next!

Josh, how you do what you do, I'll never know. Your way with spirits and knowledge is incredible, and to say that I appreciate you sharing it with me is an understatement. You, Simon, Ken, Brian, and the team at Veneto Lounge, I can't thank you enough for your support and encouragement, always. Thank you for letting me pick your brain, ask all the silly questions, and pester you about the different between yellow and green Chartreuse.

Taryn, thank you for catching our dreams, for falling in love with olive oil and vinegar, and for making the book so beautiful and vivid. If it wasn't for you and your vision, none of this would be happening. You are a rock, and you and the Touchwood team work tirelessly to bring the dream to life.

This book also wouldn't be possible without the Olive the Senses team. You are so capable and patient, and have held down the fort right from the beginning. Thank you for letting me take time to make this book happen, and for loving our customers, sharing my inspiration and passion, and running with all of it. I have learned so much from you. I love what we create together, and none of this would be possible without you, your taste buds, fridge space, and endless energy. From the chilly, outdoor staff meetings huddled around the grill, to morning check-ins that include more tapas than I care to admit, I thank you from the bottom of my heart.

INDEX

EMILY LYCOPOLUS is a recipe developer, the author of six olive oil–focused cookbooks, and a level two olive oil sommelier. She is the co-founder of eatcreative.ca, a food-driven creative content agency, and she also reviews olive oils and shares educational articles as The Olive Oil Critic at oliveoilcritic.com. Her family owns an olive grove in central Italy, where her love of olive oil began.

DANIELLE (DL) ACKEN is a Canadian-born international food photographer who splits her time between London, UK, and her farm studio on Canada's beautiful Salt Spring Island. A self-proclaimed compulsive traveler, her photography is inspired by the multitude of palettes and moods found throughout her wanderings. See her work at dlacken.com.

Edited by Lesley Cameron
Designed and illustrated by Tree Abraham
Proofread by Claire Philipson

Library and Archives Canada Cataloguing in Publication
Lycopolus, Emily, 1985-, author
Spain : recipes for olive oil and vinegar lovers / Emily Lycopolus ; photographs by DL Acken.

Includes index.

Issued in print and electronic formats.
ISBN 9781771512497 (hardcover). ISBN 9781771512503 (HTML).
ISBN 9781771512510 (PDF)

1. Cooking (Olive oil). 2. Cooking (Vinegar). 3. Olive oil. 4. Vinegar. 5. Cooking, Spanish. 6. Cookbooks. I. Title. II. Title: Recipes for olive oil & vinegar lovers.

TX819.O42L935   2018 641.6'463   C20179065572
                                                C20179065580

Canadä

We acknowledge the financial support of the Government of Canada through the Canada Book Fund and the province of British Columbia through the Book Publishing Tax Credit. This book was produced using FSC®-certified, acid-free papers, processed chlorine free, and printed with soya-based inks.

Printed in China

22   3 4 5